Marie Tarnowska

Annie Vivanti Chartres

BIBLIOLIFE

MARIE TARNOWSKA

By A. VIVANTI CHARTRES

WITH AN INTRODUCTORY LETTER
BY PROFESSOR L. M. BOSSI OF THE
UNIVERSITY OF GENOA . . . .

PUBLISHED BY THE CENTURY CO.
NEW YORK . . . . MCMXV

PREFATORY NOTE

On the morning of September 3rd, 1907, Count Paul Kamarowsky, a wealthy Russian nobleman, was fatally shot in his apartments on the Lido in Venice by an intimate friend, Nicolas Naumoff, son of the governor of Orel. The crime was at first believed to be political. The wounded man refused to make any statement against his assailant, whom he himself had assisted to escape from the balcony to a gondola in waiting below.

Count Kamarowsky was taken to a hospital, and for three days his recovery seemed assured; but the chief surgeon, in a sudden mental collapse—he has since died in an insane asylum—ordered the stitches to be removed from the fast-healing wounds, and Count Kamarowsky died in great agony a few hours later. His last words were a message of love to his betrothed at Kieff, a beautiful Russian woman, Countess Marie Tarnowska.

In her favor Count Kamarowsky had, shortly before his death, made a will and also insured his life for the sum of £20,000.

A number of telegrams from this lady were

found addressed to a Russian lawyer, Donat Prilukoff, who had been staying at the Hotel Danieli in Venice until the day of the murder. Both this man and the Countess Tarnowska were arrested.

After a sensational trial they were found guilty of instigating the young Nicolas Naumoff to commit the murder. Countess Tarnowska was sentenced to eight years' imprisonment in the penitentiary of Trani; Prilukoff was condemned to ten years' penal servitude; while Naumoff himself was liberated in view of his having undergone two years' incarceration while awaiting his trial.

TO THE AUTHOR

Signora:

Not only as the medical expert for the defense at the trial of the Countess Tarnowska, but as one who has made it his life-work to investigate the relation in women between criminal impulse and morbid physical condition, I cannot but feel the keenest interest in this book, in which you set forth the problem of wide human interest presented by the case of the prisoner of Trani.

When first I suggested to you that you should write this book—which (apart from its interest as dealing with a cause célèbre *whose protagonists are still living and well known in European society) might bring into wider knowledge doctrines that modern physiologists and psychologists are endeavoring to diffuse—you reminded me that the medical elements of the problem could not in such a work be discussed or even clearly stated. This, of course, is true, and the significance of certain indications scattered through these pages will doubtless be lost upon those who are not familiar with such matters. Nevertheless, it was important that the book should be written, for if after her release and appropriate medical treatment the Countess Tarnowska is restored, as many of us confidently anticipate, to the complete sanity of moral well-being, your book in the light of that essential fact will have fulfilled a notable mission.*

It will have helped to bring home to the general consciousness the knowledge, hitherto confined to the scientific few, that moral obliquity in women is in most cases due to pathological causes comparatively easy of diagnosis and of cure; that a woman-criminal may be morally redeemed by being physically healed; and that just as alcoholism, typhus, pyemia or other modes of toxic infection may result in delirium and irresponsibility, so certain forms of disease in women, by setting up a condition of persistent organic poisoning, may and very often do conduce to mental and moral aberration and consequent crime.

Your book, Signora, contains a truthful exposition of a group of psychic values with which physicians and psychopathists are concerned, and I believe that eventually it will promote the realization that even in the darkest regions of moral degradation it is possible for science to raise the torch of hope. Thus, though appealing for the moment to the interest of the general reader, it will ultimately constitute a significant document in the history of the evolution of pathological science.

Prof. L. M. Bossi,

Genoa,
January 12th, 1915.

TO THE READER

THIS book is not written to plead Marie Tarnowska's cause. The strange Russian woman whose hand slew no man, but whose beauty drove those who loved her to commit murder for her sake, will soon have ended her eight years' captivity and will come forth into the world once more.

I have not sought in any way to minimize her guilt, or attenuate her responsibility for the sin and death that followed in her train. Though she must be held blameless for the boy Peter Tarnowsky's tragic fate and even for Dr. Stahl's suicide, yet Bozevsky's death, Naumoff's downfall and the murder of Count Kamarowsky will forever be laid at her door.

I have tried to convey to the cool, sober mind of the Anglo-Saxon reader—to whom much of this amazing story of passion and crime may appear almost incredible—that sequence of tragic events which brought Marie Nicolaevna to her ruin.

Weighted by a heritage of disease (her mother was a neurasthenic invalid and two of her aunts are even now confined in an insane asylum in

Russia), she was married when still on the threshold of girlhood and swept into the maëlstrom of a wild life—a frenzied, almost hallucinated, existence such as is led by a certain section of the Russian aristocracy, whom self-indulgence drives to depths of degeneracy hardly to be realized by the outside world.

With the birth of her child, Tania, Marie Tarnowska's fragile health broke down completely, and the few years preceding the tragedy which led to her arrest were spent traveling through Europe in a feverish quest of health or at least of oblivion of her sufferings. According to such medical authorities as Redlich, Fenomenof, Rhein, Bossi, and many other eminent gynecologists and alienists, she is, and has been for some years past, suffering from a slow form of blood poisoning which affects the nervous centers and the brain, and which—as I myself had a painful opportunity of witnessing when I saw her in prison—causes periodic cataleptic seizures that imperil her life.

It was by one of her medical advisers, Professor Luigi Bossi, of the University of Genoa, that the idea of this book was first given to me.

"I was called as an expert for the defense at the Venice trial," said the Professor, "and I was grieved and indignant at the heavy sentence in-

flicted upon this unhappy woman. Marie Tarnowska is not delinquent, but diseased; not a
criminal, but an invalid; and her case, like that of
many other female transgressors, is one for the
surgeon's skill and the physician's compassionate
care, not for the ruthless hand of the law. Indeed,'' the illustrious Professor continued, ''it is
becoming more and more a recognized fact that
many cases of criminality in woman have a physical, not a moral origin. By her very mission—
maternity—woman is consecrated to pain; and
whereas by nature she is a creature of gentleness
and goodness, the effect of physical suffering, of
ailments often unconfessed—nay, often unrealized
by herself—is to transform her into a virago, a
hypochondriac, or a criminal. Then our duty is
to cure her, not to punish her.

''It may be merely a question,'' he explained,
''of a slight surgical intervention; sometimes even
brief medical treatment is sufficient to save a
woman's life and reason. The wider knowledge
of this simple scientific fact in the social life of our
time would redeem and rehabilitate thousands of
unfortunate women who people the prisons and
the madhouses of the world.

''As for the unhappy Countess Tarnowska,''
added Professor Bossi, ''the Venetian tribunal re-

fused to regard her as a suffering human being, but flung her out of society like some venomous reptile. Read these notes that she wrote in prison," he said, placing in my hand a book of almost illegible memoranda. "If they touch your heart, then do a deed of justice and generosity. Go to the penitentiary of Trani, see the prisoner yourself, and give her story to the world. So will you perform an act of humanity and beneficence by helping to diffuse a scientific truth in favor, not of this one woman alone, but of all women."

After glancing through the strange human document he had given me I decided to do what he asked; for, indeed, from those poor, incoherent pages there seemed to rise the eternal cry of suffering womanhood—the anguished cry of those that perpetuate the gift of life—which no sister-soul can hear unmoved.

Thus it was that my mind was first directed to the theme of this book and that I undertook the task—fraught with almost insuperable difficulties —of breaking down official prohibitions and reaching the Russian captive in her distant Italian prison.

And now that I have been brought face to face with that strange and mournful figure, now that I have heard her story from her own pale lips, I

am moved by the puissant impulse of art, which
takes no heed of learned theory or ethical code,
to narrate in these pages the profound impression
made upon me by that tragic personality, by the
story of that broken life.

I have endeavored to do so with faithfulness,
exaggerating nothing, coloring nothing, extenuat-
ing nothing. It will be for the pontiffs of science
and morals to achieve the more complex task of
drawing conclusions and establishing theories that
may one day diminish injustice and suffering in
the world.

A. VIVANTI CHARTRES.

LIST OF ILLUSTRATIONS

Facing page

MARIE NICOLAEVNA TARNOWSKA . *Frontispiece*

A PAGE FROM MARIE TARNOWSKA'S NOTE-BOOK . 6

COUNT O'ROURKE 20

COUNT PAUL KAMAROWSKY 180

I STEPPED OUT UPON THE BALCONY 194

UNDER ARREST 268

IN THE PRISON CELL 292

THE PENITENTIARY AT TRANI 300

MARIE TARNOWSKA

MARIE TARNOWSKA

I

Ed or, che Dio mi tolga la memoria.
CONTESSA LARA.

THE verdant landscape of Tuscany swung past the train that carried me southward. The looped vineyards—like slim, green dancers holding hands —fled backwards as we passed, and the rays of the March sun pursued us, beating hotly through the open windows on the dusty red velvet cushions of the carriage.

Soon the train was throbbing and panting out of Pisa, and the barefooted children of the Roman Campagna stood to gaze after us, with eyes soft and wild under their sullen hair.

Since leaving the station of Genoa I had seen nothing of the fleeting springtide landscape; my gaze and thoughts were riveted on the pages of a copy-book which lay open on my knee—a simple school copy-book with innocent blue-lined

3

sheets originally intended to contain the carefully
labored scrawls of some childish hand. A blue
ornamental flourish decked the front; and under
the printed title, "Program of Lessons," the
words "History," "Geography," "Arithmetic,"
were followed by a series of blank spaces for the
hours to be filled in. Alas, for the tragic pupil to
whom this book belonged, in what school of horror had she learned the lesson traced on these
pages by her slim, white hand—the fair patrician
hand which had known the weight of many jewels,
the thrill of many caresses, and was now held fast
in the merciless grip of captivity.

I turned the page: before me lay a flow of pale
penciled words in a sloping handwriting. At
every turn the flourish of some strange seignorial
name met my eye: long Russian names of prince,
of lover or of murderer. On every page was the
convulsion of death or the paroxysm of passion;
wine and morphia, chloral and cocaine surged
across the pallid sheets, like the wash of a nightmare sea.

From the midst of those turbid billows—like
some ineffable modern Aphrodite—rose the pale
figure of Marie Nicolaevna Tarnowska.

The first words—traced by her trembling hand

in the prison at Venice—are almost childish in their simplicity.

"When I was eight years old, I fell ill with measles and almost lost my eyesight. I wore blue spectacles. I was very happy. My mother loved me very much; so did my father. So did the servants. Everybody loved me very much."

I pause in my reading, loth to proceed. I wish I could stop here with the little girl whom every one loved and who gazed out through her blue spectacles at a rose-colored world.

Ah! Marie Nicolaevna, had your luminous eyes remained for all time hidden behind those dim blue glasses, no one to-day would raise his voice in execration of you, nor call anathema upon your fair bowed head.

But when the little Russian countess was twelve years old an oculist from Kieff ordered that her eyes should be uncovered, and "Mura," as her parents fondly called her, looked out upon the world with those clear light eyes that were one day to penetrate the darkest depths of crime.

I continue to read without stopping. The serried pages, scrawled feverishly and hurriedly in the cells of La Giudecca in defiance of prison rules, are in thin handwriting, with names and dates harshly underlined; but here and there whole sentences are struck out, as if the writer's memory wavered, or her feelings altered as she wrote.

Immediately, on the very first page, the bold figure of young Vassili Tarnowsky confronts us: the radiant, temerarious lover, who came to woo her in her marveling adolescence.

"His voice thrilled the heart like the tones of a violoncello; in his eyes were the lights of heaven, in his smile all the promises of love. I was already seventeen years old, and wise beyond my years. But, sagacious as I thought myself, I could never believe anything that was told me against Vassili. My eyes saw nothing but his beauty. On the twelfth day of April I ran away from home with him; and we were married in a little church far away on the desolate steppes. I never thought that life could hold such joy."

But on the very next page we come face to face with the astounding list of Vassili's perfidies: a musical enumeration of feminine names which rings the knell of his child-wife's happiness. "I never thought," writes Marie Tarnowska simply, "that life could hold such sorrow."

Further on there are gaps and incoherences; here and there a passing efflorescence of literary phrase, or a sudden lapse into curt narrative, as if a wave of apathy had suddenly submerged the tragic heroine and left in her place only a passive narrator of fearful events. Now and then even a note of strident humor is struck, more poignant, more painful than pathos.

Ever and anon there appears throughout the funereal story—as if smiling out through the window of a charnel-house—the innocent face of a child: Tioka. He is all bright curls and laughter. Unaware of the carnage that surrounds him, he runs with light, quick feet through pools of blood to nestle in the gentle maternal breast which for him is all purity and tenderness.

.   .   .   .

As I read on and on the writing trembles and wavers, as if the hand and the heart of the writer wearied of their task. With a sudden break the sad story closes, unfinished, incomplete.

"If I could tell of the tears I have shed, if I could describe the anguish I have suffered, I am sure that pity would be shown to me. Surely if the world knew of my torment and my sufferings—"

Nothing more. Thus abruptly the tragic manuscript ends.

The train slackens speed, falters, shivers—

stops. I am at Trani; at the furthermost end of Italy; almost beyond civilization; almost out of the world.

Soon I shall see before me the woman I have come so far to seek: the woman who never gave the gift of love without the gift of death.

The high white walls of the penitentiary glared down in the blazing southern sun. The languid Adriatic trailed its blue silken waters past the barred windows. I raised the heavy knocker; it fell from my hand with a reverberating clang, and the massive prison-door opened slowly before me.

The Mother Superior and two gentle-looking Sisters fluttered—black and white and timid as swallows—across the sunlit courtyard. They were expecting me.

"She whom you seek is in the chapel," said the Mother Superior, in a low voice. "I will call her!" She left us. The two Sisters accompanied me up a broad stone staircase to a small waiting-room. Then they stood quietly beside me; and when I looked at them, they smiled.

In the silence that followed I could hear women's voices singing in the prison chapel, simple, untutored voices, clear and shrill:

"Kyrie eleison
Christe eleison . . ."

and the low notes of the organ rolled beneath the treble voices, full and deep:

"Mater purissima
Mater inviolata . . ."

"Number 315—that is the Countess Marie," said one of the two Sisters, "plays the organ for the other prisoners. She plays every day at noon and evensong."

"And at four o'clock in the morning," added the other Sister.

(How far, how far away, Marie Nicolaevna, are the passionate days of Moscow, the glowing, unslept nights of Venice!)

"Rosa mystica
Stella matutina . . ."

Suddenly the music ceased and we stood waiting in the hot, white silence. Then the door opened, and on the threshold stood Marie Tarnowska—the murderess, the devastating spirit, the Erinnys.

II

TALL and motionless in her fearful striped dress she stood, gazing at me with proud clear eyes; her brow was calm and imperious under the humiliating prisoner's coif, and her long hands—those delicate hands whose caresses have driven men to commit murder for her sake—hung loosely at her side. Her mouth, curving and disdainful, trembled slightly.

"Signora," I began. Her lips wavered into a faint smile as with a quick downward sweep of her eyelashes she indicated her dress of shame.

"Signora," I repeated, "I have come here neither out of compassion nor curiosity."

She was silent, waiting for me to proceed. The three nuns had seated themselves quietly near the wall, with eyes cast down and meek hands folded in their laps.

"I have come," I continued, "to vindicate my sisters in your eyes. I know you think that all women are ruthless and unkind."

Another smile, fleeting, vivid and intelligent, lit

10

up her eyes. Then the narrow face closed and darkened again.

"For two years," I proceeded, "I have been haunted by the thought that you, shut in this place, must be saying to yourself that all men are base and all women pitiless. As to the men—I cannot say. But I wish you to know that not all women are without pity."

She was silent a few moments. Then in a weak voice she spoke:

"In the name of how many women do you bring this message to me?"

I smiled in my turn. "There are four of us," I said, cheerfully. "Two Englishwomen, a Norwegian, who is deaf and dumb—and myself. The deaf and dumb one," I added, "is really very intelligent."

Marie Tarnowska laughed! It was a low, sudden trill of laughter, and she herself seemed startled at the unaccustomed sound. The Sisters turned to look at her with an air of gentle amazement.

But in my eyes Marie Tarnowska had ceased to be the murderess, the Erinnys. Through the criminal in her dress of shame I had caught a glimpse of the little girl in the blue spectacles, the happy little girl who felt that every one loved her.

That lonely, tremulous trill of laughter astray on the tragic lips stirred me to the depths; and sudden tears filled my eyes.

Marie Tarnowska saw this, and turned pale. Then she sat down, unconsciously assuming the same chastened attitude as the Sisters, her hands submissively folded, her dark lashes cast down over her long light eyes. For some time there was silence.

"I have read your notes," I said at last.

"My notes? I do not remember writing them." Suddenly her voice sounded harsh and her glance flashed at me keen as a blade of steel.

"You wrote them in the prison at Venice, in pencil, in a child's exercise book."

"It may be so." Marie Tarnowska breathed a long sigh. "That was a time of dreams," she said, raising her stricken eyes to mine. "I sometimes dream that this is all a dream. I think I must have fallen asleep one day when I was a little child, at home in Otrada—perhaps in our garden on the swing. I used often to fall asleep on that creaky old swing, reading a book, or looking at the sky. Perhaps I shall wake up soon, and find that none of all these dreadful things are true." She fingered the broad brown-and-white stripes of her prison-garb and gazed round the dreary room. Then her eyes strayed from the whitewashed walls, bare except for a large ebony crucifix, to the narrow iron-barred window, and back to the Sisters sitting along the wall like a triptych of Renunciation, with folded hands and lips moving silently in their habitual prayer. "Yes, I shall wake up soon and find myself in our old garden again. My mother will come down the path and across the lawn, with her little white shawl on her head; she will call me: 'Mura! Mura! Where are you? Come, child, it is time for tea; and Vassili is asking for you.' Then I shall jump from the swing and run to her and hide my face on her breast. 'Mother, if you knew what a dream I have had—a terrible dream, all about deaths and murders! I thought I had married Vassili, and he was unkind to me—as if Vassili could be unkind!—and I was locked in a prison in Italy—imagine, mother, to be imprisoned in Italy, where people only go for their honeymoon!' And mother will kiss me and laugh at the crazy dream as we go across the lawn together, happily, arm in arm."

I found no word to say, though her eyes seemed to question me; and her fragile voice spoke again: "Surely, this cannot all be true? It cannot be true that they are all dead. My mother? And little Peter? And Bozevsky? And Stahl? And Kamarowsky? Why, it is like—like 'Hamlet.'" She broke into strident laughter. "Do you remember how they all die in 'Hamlet'? One here, one there, one in the stream, one behind the curtain, drowned, stabbed, strangled—" Suddenly she was silent, looking straight before her with startled eyes.

"Poor Mura!" I murmured, and lightly touched her hand.

At the sound of the tender Russian appellative she turned to me quickly. Then she began speaking under her breath in hurried whispers.

"Who told you my name? Who are you? Are you my sister Olga? Do you remember the merry-go-round at the school-feast in Kieff? How we cried when it swung us round and round and round and would not stop? I seem to be still on the merry-go-round, rushing along, hastening, hurrying with the loud music pealing in my head."

The Mother Superior rose and approached her. "Hush," she spoke in soothing tones. "You will soon be quiet and at rest."

But Marie Tarnowska paid no heed. Her eyes were still fixed on mine with a despairing gaze. "Wake me, wake me!" she cried. "And let me tell you my dream."

And during those long mild April days she told it to me as follows.

Where shall I begin? Wait, let me think—ah, yes! Where I fell asleep that day in the garden, on the swing. I remember it was a hot day even in Otrada; almost as hot as it is here. And it was my birthday; I was sixteen years old. My mother herself, with great solemnity, in the presence of my father and sisters, had twisted up my long curling hair and pinned it in great waves and coils on the top of my head. There were to be no more long plaits hanging down my back!

"Your childhood is over, Mura," said my mother. "At sixteen one has to look and behave like a grown-up young lady."

"That is exactly what I am, mother dear," I replied with great self-assurance.

My mother smiled and sighed and kissed me. "You are such a child—such a child still, my little snowdrop," she said, and her eyes were tender and anxious.

But I ran gaily out into the garden, feeling very proud of my red-gold helmet of curls. I sprang fearlessly on the swing, tossing my head from side to side, delighted to feel the back of my neck cool and uncovered to the breeze. What would Vassili say to see me like this! But soon the hair-

pins felt heavy; they pulled a hair or two here,
and a hair or two there, and hurt me. I stopped
the swing, and with my head bent forward I
quickly drew all the hairpins out and threw them
on the ground.

The heavy coils of hair loosened, untwisted like
a glittering snake, and fell all about me like a cloak
of gold. I leaped upon the swing again and,
standing, swung myself in wide flights through
the clear air. What joy it was! As I flew forward my hair streamed out behind me like a flag,
and in the backward sweep it floated all about my
head in a whirling canopy of light.

I laughed and sang out loud to myself. How delightful was the world! How blissful to be alive
and in the sunshine!

Suddenly Vassili appeared at the end of the path
with my cousin, Prince Troubetzkoi. They were
coming towards me arm in arm, smoking cigarettes and gazing at me. I felt shy of my loosened
hair; I should have liked to jump down and run
away, but the swing was flying too high and I could
not stop it.

The two men looked at me with strange intent
eyes, as no one had ever looked at me before. I
felt a hot blush rise to my cheeks like a flame.
Obeying a sudden, overmastering impulse I let go

the ropes and covered my face with my hands.
I heard a cry—did it come from me?—then everything whirled round me. . . . For an instant I saw
the gravel path rise straight in front of me as if
to strike me on the forehead. I threw myself
back, something seemed to crash into the nape of
my neck—and I remember no more.

III

I SEE the ensuing days as through a vague blue
mist. I see myself reclining in an armchair, and
my mother sitting beside me with her crochet-
work. She is crocheting something of yellow
wool. It is strange how the sight of that yellow
wool hurts and repels me, but I cannot find words
in which to express it, I seem unable to speak;
and mother crochets on calmly, with quick white
hands. I am conscious of a dull pain in the nape
of my neck. Then I see Vassili come in; he is
carrying an enormous cage in his hand; and Olga
follows him, laughing and radiant. "Here he is!
here he is!" cries Vassili triumphantly, putting
the cage down beside me; and in it, to my horror,
I see a parrot, a huge gray and scarlet creature,
twisting a hard black tongue round and round as
he clambers about the cage. I cry out in terror:
"Why—why do they bring me things that frighten
me?" And I burst into tears. Every one gazes
at me in amazement; my mother bends tenderly
over me: "But, my own darling, yesterday you
said you wanted to have a parrot. Vassili has
been all the way to Moscow to buy it for you."

"No, no! it is not true! I never said I wanted a parrot! Take it away! It frightens me. And so does the yellow wool." I hear myself weeping loudly; then everything is blotted out and vanishes —parrot, Vassili, yellow wool, Olga—nothing remains but my mother's sad and anxious face bending above me, dim and constant as the light of a lamp in a shadowy chapel.

When I was able to come down to breakfast for the first time, my father stood waiting for me, straight and solemn at the foot of the great staircase. He gave me his arm with much ceremony and led me to my place, where flowers lay in fragrant heaps round my plate. Every one embraced and complimented me and I was very happy.

"I feel as if I were a princess!" I cried, clapping my hands; and they all laughed except my father, who answered gravely:

"If it is your wish, you may become one. Prince Ivan has asked for your hand."

"Ivan? Ivan Troubetzkoi?" All the gladness went out of my heart.

"Yes. And so has Katerinowitch," exclaimed Olga, with a bitter smile; and I noticed that she looked pale and sad.

"Both Ivan and Katerinowitch? How extraordinary!'' Then glancing at my mother, whose eyes were fixed upon her plate, I added jestingly, ''Is that all? No one else?''

My pleasantry fell flat, for no one answered, and I saw my father knitting his brows. But my mother lifted her eyes for an instant and looked at me. In the blue light of that dear gaze I read my happiness!

But Olga was speaking. ''Yes,'' she said, ''there is some one else. Vassili Tarnowsky has asked to marry you.'' And she added, with a touch of bitterness: ''I wonder what has possessed all three of them!''

Vassili! Vassili! Vassili! The name rang like a clarion in my ears. I should be Vassili's wife! I should be the Countess Tarnowska—the happiest woman in all this happy world. Every other girl on earth—poor luckless girls who could not marry Vassili—would envy me. On his arm I should pass proudly and serenely through life, rejoicing in his beauty, protected by his strength. Sheltered on his breast the storms would pass over my head, nor could sorrow ever touch me.

''I trust that your choice will fall on Troubetzkoi,'' said my father.

''Or on Vassili,'' cried Olga quickly.

I jumped up and embraced her. ''It shall not

COUNT O'ROURKE

be Katerinowitch, that I promise," I whispered, kissing the little pink ear that nestled under her fair curls. "He is to be for you!"

Time was to fulfil this prophecy.

As I went round the table, and passed my mother —poor little nervous mother!—I laid my hand on her arm. I noticed that she was trembling all over. Then I summoned up courage and approached my father.

"Father, dear, if you want your little Mura to be happy, you must let her marry Vassili."

"Never," cried my father, striking the table with his fist. The soul of the ancient O'Rourke— a demoniacal Irish ancestor of ours whose memory always struck terror to our souls—had awakened in him. I saw Olga and my mother turn pale. Nevertheless I laughed and kissed him again. "If I do not marry Vassili, I shall die! And please, father, do not be the Terrible O'Rourke, for you are frightening mother!"

But papa, dominated by the atavistic influence of the O'Rourke, grew even more terrible; and mother was greatly frightened. She sat white and rigid, with scarcely fluttering breath; suddenly in her transparent eyes the pupils floated upward like two misty pale-blue half-moons; she was in the throes of one of her dreaded epileptic seizures.

Then they were all around her, helping her, loosening her dress, fanning her; while I stood aside trembling and woebegone, and the pains in the nape of my neck racked me anew.

I said to myself that my father was hard and wicked, that I should marry Vassili and carry mother off with me, ever so far away!

As for papa, he should only be allowed to see us once a year. At Christmas.

.   .   .   .

I have married Vassili.

I pretended to be seized with such convulsions that my poor dear mother, being at her wits' end, at last allowed me to run away with him.

Do I say "I pretended"? I am not sure that that is correct. At first the convulsions were certainly a mere pretense. I would say to myself: "Now I shall make myself have convulsions." But as soon as I had begun I could not stop. After I had voluntarily gnashed my teeth they seemed to become locked as in a vice; my fists that I had purposely clenched would not reopen. My nails dug into the palms of my hands, and I could see the blood flowing down my wrists without being able to unclasp or relax my fingers.

Doctor Orlof, summoned in haste from Kieff, shook his head gravely.

"There are indications of epilepsy, due to the fall from the swing."

"No, no, no!" I cried. "Not the swing! It is because of Vassili!"

My mother trembled and wept.

How cruel we are in our childhood! How we torture the mothers that adore us, even though we love them with all our hearts. And oh! the tragedy of not understanding this until it is too late, when we can never, never ask for their forgiveness, nor console them or atone to them again.

I married Vassili.

My father, more the Terrible O'Rourke than ever, at once refused to have anything to do with me. He denied me his kiss and his forgiveness. I was very unhappy.

"Oh, don't bother your head about that tiresome old man," said Vassili, much annoyed by my tears.

As for my mother, she could only entreat Vassili to be kind and gentle with me.

"Take care of her, Vassili," she implored. "I have given her to you lest she should die of a broken heart: but she is really too young to be any one's wife—she is but a child! I do not know whether you understand me. Remember she is not yet a woman. She is a child.''

''Yes, yes, yes,'' said Vassili, without paying much attention. ''That 's all right. I shall tweak her nose if she is naughty.''

''And if I am good?'' I asked, lifting ecstatic eyes to his handsome nonchalant face.

''If you are good you shall have sweets and kisses!'' and he laughed, showing all his white teeth.

''Promise me, Vassili, that you will always sing my favorite song: 'Oh distant steppes, oh savage plains,' to me, and to no one else.''

''To you and to no one else,'' said Vassili with mock solemnity. ''Come then, Marie Tarnowska!'' and he drew my arm under his, patting my hand on which the new nuptial ring shone in all its brightness.

''*Marie Tarnowska!*'' What a beautiful name! I could have wished the whole world to know that name; I could have wished that every one seeing me should say: ''Behold, behold Marie Tarnowska, happiest and most blessed among women.''

IV

On my wedding night, in the hotel at Kharkoff, I summoned the chambermaid. She knocked and entered. She was a pert, pretty creature, and after surveying me from head to foot she threw a rapid glance at Vassili. He was seated in an armchair, lighting a cigarette.

"What is your name?" he asked the girl.

"Rosalia, at your service, sir," she replied.

"Very good, Rosalia," said my husband. "This evening we shall do without you. Possibly in a day or two I may wish to see you again."

The girl laughed, made a slight curtsey, and went out, closing the door behind her.

"But who is going to do my hair?" I asked, feeling very much out of countenance and shy at remaining alone with him.

"Never mind about your hair," said Vassili. "Don't be so tedious. You 're a little bore." And he kissed me.

Then he sat down and smoked his cigarette, watching me out of narrowed eyelids as I wandered about the room in great trepidation and embarrassment. I was about to kneel down by the bedside to say my prayers, when he suddenly grasped my wrist and held it tightly.

"What are you doing now?" he inquired.

"I am going to say my prayers," I replied.

"Don't bother about your prayers," he said. "Try not to be such an awful little bore. Really you are quite insufferable."

But I would not have missed my prayers for the world. At home prayers had always been a matter of great importance. Olga and I used to say them aloud in unison morning and evening. And now that Olga was far away I must say them alone. I buried my face in my hands and said them devoutly, with all my heart.

They were, I admit, numerous and long; and they were in many languages, for every nurse or governess that came to us in Otrada had taught us new ones; and Olga and I were afraid to leave any out, lest God should be offended; we were also rather doubtful as to which language He understood the best.

I had just come to an English prayer—

> Now I lay me down to sleep
> I pray Thee, Lord, my soul to keep.
> If I should die before I wake . . .

(Here Olga and I used always to interpolate a short prayer of our own invention: "Please, dear

God, do not on any account let us die to-night. Amen.'')—when Vassili interrupted me.

"Haven't you finished?'' he cried, putting his arm round my neck. "You are very tiresome. You bore me to extinction.''

"You bore me!'' That was the perpetual refrain of all his days. I always bored him. Perhaps it was not surprising. At seventeen one is not always clever and entertaining, especially outside the family circle. At home I had always been considered rather witty and intelligent, but to Vassili I was never anything but "a dreadful bore.''

When I caught sight of him pinching Rosalia's cheek and I burst into tears: "You are a fearful bore,'' he said crossly. If I noticed the scent of musk or patchouli on his coat and ventured to question him about it—"You are an insufferable little bore,'' would be all the answer I got. When he went out (taking the music of "My Savage Plains'' with him) and stayed away all night, on his return next morning I sobbed out my anguish on his breast. "I must say you bore me to death,'' he yawned.

And one day I heard that he had had a child by a German baroness.

At the sight of my paroxysm of despair he grew

angry. "What does it matter to you, silly creature, since you have not got one yourself?" he exclaimed. "Wearisome little bore that you are; you can't even have a child."

I was aghast. What—what did he mean? Why could I not—?

"No! no!" he shouted, with his handsome mouth rounded and open like those of the stone cherubs on the walls of his castle, "you will never have any children. You are not a woman. Your mother herself said so." And the look which he flashed across my frail body cut me like a sword.

I fell fainting to the ground.

Then he became alarmed. He called everybody. He summoned the whole staff of the hotel. He sent for all the ladies he knew in Kharkoff (and they were many) imploring them all to save me, to recall me to life. When I came to myself the room was filled with women: there was Rosalia, and two Hungarian girls from the adjoining apartment, and there was also the German baroness, and little Julia Terlezkaja, the latest and fairest of my husband's conquests. All these graceful creatures were bending over my couch, while Vassili on his knees with his head buried in the coverlet was sobbing: "Save her! She is dead! I have killed her!"

I put out my hand and touched his hair.

"I am alive," I said softly; and he threw himself upon me and kissed me. The women stood round us in a semi-circle, gay and graceful as the figures on a Gobelin tapestry.

"I love you," Vassili was exclaiming; "I love you just as you are. I should hate you to be like everybody else." And in French he added, looking at Madame Terlezkaja: "C'est très rigolo d'avoir une femme qui n'est pas une femme."

I hid my face in the pillow, and wept; while the fair Terlezkaja, who seemed to be the kindest of them all, bent over and consoled me.

"Pay no heed to him," she whispered. "I think he has been drinking a little."

The door opened. A doctor, who had been sent for by the manager of the hotel, entered with a resolute authoritative air. At the sight of him the women disappeared like a flight of startled sparrows. Of course they took Vassili with them.

To the good old doctor I confided the secret which Vassili had disclosed to me and which was burning my heart.

"I want to have a child, a little child of my own!" I cried.

"Of course. Of course. So you shall," said the old doctor, with a soothing smile. "There is no reason why you should not. You are a little anemic, that is all."

He scribbled some prescriptions on his tablets.

"There. You will take all that. And you will go to Franzensbad. Within a year you will be asking me to act as godpapa."

I took all he prescribed. But I did not go to Franzensbad. Vassili wanted to go to Petersburg, so, of course, it was to Petersburg we went.

The very first evening we were there a number of his friends came to call on him.

I remember, among the rest, a certain German Grand Duke, who, after showing me an infinite amount of attention, drew Vassili aside and spoke to him in undertones. I heard him mention the name of a famous restaurant and the words: "A jolly supper-party to-night—some ravishingly pretty tziganes . . ." There followed names of men and women whom I did not know, and my husband laughed loudly.

Then the Grand Duke turned to me, and bowing deeply and ceremoniously kissed my hand.

For an instant a frenzied impulse came over me to clutch that well-groomed head and cry: "Wicked man! Why are you trying to lure my husband from me?" But social conventions prevailed over this elementary instinct, and when the

Grand Duke raised his patrician head he found me all amiability and smiles.

"She is indeed a bewitching creature!" I heard him mutter to Vassili. "Looks just like one of Botticelli's diaphanous angels. Well then, at eleven o'clock to-night, at the 'Hermitage.'"

Promptly at a quarter to eleven Vassili, sleek, trim and immaculate, kissed my cheek gaily and went out.

I was alone. Alone in the great drawing-room, gorgeous with lights and mirrors and gilded decorations. What was the good of being a be-witching creature? What was the good of looking like one of Botticelli's diaphanous angels? . . .

V

I RANG for my maid, Katja, a good creature, ugly
beyond words—and gladly chosen by me on that
account—and I told her that she was to undress
me for I was going to bed. While she was unfas-
tening my dress I could hear her muttering: "If
it were me, I should not go to bed. If it were me,
I should put on my diamonds and my scarlet chiffon gown; I should take a good bottle of vitriol in
my pocket, and go and see what they were up to."

"Katja, what are you mumbling? Do you mean
to say that you—that you think I ought to go—?"

"Of course," she cried, and her small squinting
eyes shot forth, to the right and left, fierce, di-
vergent flashes of indignation. "Why should my
lady not go?"

Why should I not, indeed? Had I not the right
—nay, the duty—to follow Vassili? Had I not
most solemnly promised so to do, in the little
church on the steppes a year ago? *"Follow
him!"* With what tremulous joy had I repeated
after the priest those two words of tenacity and
submission. Had they no application to the
Hermitage restaurant?

"Perhaps I might venture to go," I murmured, "but, Katja, do not other women always have rouge and powder to put on when they go out? I have nothing."

"Nothing but your eighteen years, madame," replied Katja.

She dressed me in the low-necked scarlet chiffon gown. She drew on my flame-colored stockings, and my crimson shoes. On my head she placed the diamond and ruby tiara, and about my shoulders she wound a red and gold scarf which looked like a snake of fire.

"Alas, Katja!" I sighed as I looked at myself in the mirror; "what would my mother say if she were to see me like this? What do I look like?"

"You look like a lighted torch," said Katja.

I made her come with me in the troika, which sped swiftly and silently through the dim snow-covered streets. I was shaking with fear at the thought of Vassili. Katja was mumbling some prayers.

We drew up at the brilliant entrance of the restaurant.

"Oh, heavens, Katja! What will my husband say?"

"He will say that you are beautiful."

How did I ever venture across that threshold of

dazzling light? How was I able to ascend the red-carpeted stairs, preceded and followed by bows and smiles and whispers? At the head of the wide staircase, in front of a double-paneled door of white and gold, I paused with beating heart, almost unable to breathe. I could hear the gipsy-music inside, and women's voices and men's laughter and the tinkling of glasses.

An impassive head-waiter stood before me, calmly awaiting my orders.

"Tell"—I stammered—"tell—" as I thought of Vassili my courage failed me—"tell his Highness the Grand Duke that I wish to see him."

Then I clung to the balustrade and waited. As the door opened and was quickly closed again, there came forth a puff of heat and sound which enwrapped me like a flame.

Almost immediately the door opened again and the Grand Duke appeared upon the threshold, his countenance still elated by recent laughter. He stared at me in astonishment, without recognition. "What—what can I do for you?" he asked. Then his eyes widened in limitless astonishment. "Upon my word! It is the Botticelli angel!"

I said "Yes," and felt inclined to weep.

"Come in, come in!" he cried eagerly, taking me by the arm and leading me to the door.

A waiter threw it wide open. I had a dazzling vision of a table resplendent with crystal, silver, and flowers, and the bare jeweled shoulders of women.

"Tarnowsky!" called the Grand Duke from the threshold. "Fortunate among men! Behold—the most glorious of your conquests!"

Vassili had started to his feet and was looking at me with amazed and incredulous eyes. There was a deep silence. I felt as if I should die. Vassili came up to me. He took me brusquely by the hand, crushing my fingers in his iron clasp. "You are mad!" he said. Then he looked at me from head to foot—not with the gaze of a husband, nor yet with that of a lover, but with the cold curious scrutiny of the perfect connoisseur.

"Come," he said at last, drawing me towards the others who were in a riot of laughter. "I have always told my friends that you were a chilling, lily-white flake of snow. You are not!" And he laughed. "You are a blazing little firebrand! Come in!"

Thenceforward my husband would always have me with him. My untutored adolescence was trailed from revelry to revelry, from banquet to orgy; my innocence swept into the maelstrom of a licentious life. I was forced to look into the depths of every depravity; to my lips was proffered every chalice of shame.

Oh, if as I stood trembling on the confines of maidenhood, some strong and tender hand had drawn me into safety, should not I have been like other women, those happy women who walk with lofty brows in the sunshine, august and ruthless in their purity?

But, alas! when with tardy and reluctant step I issued forth from my long childhood, a thousand cruel hands were thrust out to push me towards the abyss.

Oh, white pathway of innocence which knows no return! Oh, tenuous light of purity which, once quenched, kindles no more! Did I not grieve and mourn for you when I lost you before my twentieth year? Sadly, enviously, like some poor exile, I saw other girls of my age passing in blithe security by the side of their mothers, blushing at an eager word or at a daring glance. Alas! I felt that I was unworthy to kiss the hem of their skirts.

But bliss was to be vouchsafed to me. Redeeming and triumphant there came to me at last the Angel of Maternity. With proud humility I bore the little human flower fluttering in my breast.

At every throb of life I felt myself swooning with joy—with the ineffable joy of my reconquered purity.

My mother was with me, and in the tender haven of her arms I found shelter for my meek and boundless ecstasy.

How is it possible, I asked myself, that there are women who dread this perfect happiness, who weep and suffer through these months fraught with rapturous two-fold life?

For me, I felt like a flowering plant in spring-time, impelled by some potent influence towards its perfect blossoming. The whole of that blissful period seemed a sublime ascent to unalloyed felicity; everything enchanted me, from the awed and tremulous waiting to the final crowning consummation.

When at last the fragile infant—my son!—lay in my arms, he seemed to me sufficient to fill my entire life. I nursed him into ever-growing wonder and beauty. Day by day he seemed fairer, more entrancing, like a delicate flower in some fantastic lunar legend.

Oh, the wee groping hands against my face! The wilful little caprices, the cries like those of an angry dove! And the dimples on the elbows; the droll battle with the little cap always awry, and the joyous impatience of the tiny kicking feet!

Each day my mother and I invented new names for him—names of little flowers, names of little animals, nonsense-names made up of sweet senseless sounds.

I had no thought, I had no desire. Pale and pure I sat enthroned in the milk-white paradise of maternity.

VI

Soon after that my thoughts are adrift, my recollections grow confused. I see my mother with my baby in her arms, and myself in traveling attire, with my arms twined about them, weeping, despairing, refusing to leave them and set out on a journey of Vassili's planning. But Vassili grows impatient. Vassili grows angry. He is tired of playing the papa, tired of seeing me no longer a little "firebrand," but calm as a young Madonna in the beatific purity of motherhood.

Vassili has taken it into his head that he wants to study singing. He has made up his mind to go to Italy, to Milan, to study scales and exercises; and I must go with him.

"But our baby, Vassili, our little Tioka! We must take our baby with us!"

No. Vassili does not want babies. He does not want to be bothered or hindered. "We are carting about eight trunks as it is!" he says, cynically.

And so we start for Italy—Italy, the yearned-for goal of all my girlish dreams.

At Milan Vassili sings. I seem always to see

him with his handsome mouth open, singing scales and arpeggios. But a slow poison is creeping through my blood and I fall ill, ill with typhoid fever.

Again my thoughts go adrift and my recollections are confused. They dance in grotesque and hideous visions through my brain. I see livid hallucinated faces peering at me, towers and mountains tottering above me, undefined horrors all about me, and in the midst of them all I see Vassili—singing! He sings scales and arpeggios with his rounded open mouth. Now I can see a white spider—no, two white spiders—running about on a scarlet coverlet. . . . They are my hands. They frighten me. And Vassili is singing.

"Vassili, why are you singing? Don't sing! Don't sing!"

"No, darling, I am not singing. You only imagine it. You are ill; you are feverish. Calm yourself."

.   .   .   .

"Vassili, where is my baby?"

"At home in Kieff, with grandmama. Dear grandmama is taking such good care of him!"

"And why are we not with him? Where are we?"

"We are at Pegli, darling."

"Why? Why? Where is Pegli? What are we doing at Pegli?"

"Come now, dearest; you know—we came to Italy because I wanted to sing—"

"Ah, you see! You wanted to sing! Why do you want to sing when the baby is crying? The baby is so helpless. Why did you take me away from him? You sing, you sing so loud that I cannot hear my baby crying. Don't sing!"

But even as I speak I see that Vassili has his round mouth open again and he sings and sings, and the white spiders run over the scarlet counterpane and come close to my face—and the white spiders are my hands. I shriek and shriek to have them taken away. But the baby is crying and Vassili is singing and no one hears me.

.   .   .   .

Then I drop down to the bottom of a deep well. I feel myself falling, falling, until with a great shock I touch the bottom. And there I lie motionless in the dark.

.   .   .   .

When I open my eyes there is a great deal of light; the windows are open, the sun is pouring in; I know that outside there is the sea. Beside my bed sits a doctor with a gray beard, feeling my pulse. Under the light intermittent pressure of his fingers my pulse seems to grow quieter; I can see the doctor's head giving little nods as he counts the beats.

"Sixty-five. Excellent, excellent!" The doctor pats my hand gently and encouragingly. "That is first-rate. We are quite well again."

Then I hear some one weeping softly, and I know it is my mother. I try to turn and smile at her, but my head will not move. It is like a ball of lead sunk in the pillow. Immediately afterwards—or have years passed?—I hear some one say: "Here is the Professor!" And again the same doctor with the gray beard comes in and smiles at me.

Before sitting down beside the bed he turns to my mother: "Has she not yet asked about her child?" My mother shakes her head and presses her handkerchief to her eyes. Then the doctor sits down beside my bed and strokes my forehead and speaks to me.

He speaks about a baby. He repeats a name over and over again—perhaps it is Tioka. Tioka? Who is Tioka? I watch his beard moving up and down, and do not know what he is saying. The ball of lead on my pillow rolls from side to side with a dull and heavy ache.

My mother weeps bitterly: "Oh, doctor, do not let her die!"

The white spiders are there again, running over the coverlet. And I fall once more, down, down, down, to the bottom of the well.

VII

FOR how many months was I ill? I do not know. Vassili, restless and idle, "carted" me and my medicines and my sufferings from Pegli to Genoa, from Genoa to Florence. He seemed to have forgotten that we had a home; he seemed to have forgotten that we had a child.

Our rooms at the hotel in Florence were bright with sunshine and with the frivolous gaiety of a graceful trio of Russian ladies—the Princess Dubinskaja, her sister Vera Vojatschek, and the fair-haired Olga Kralberg, who came to see us every day. But I felt lost and lonely, as if astray in the world. My mother had returned to Russia, and my vacant and aching heart invoked Vassili, who, alas! was never by my side.

"You must win him back," said Olga Kralberg to me one day—she, whose fate it was on a not distant day to commit suicide for his sake. "Every man, especially if he is a husband, has —after some time—to be won back again."

"That is sooner said than done," I replied despondently. "To win a man is easy enough. But to win him back—"

"There are various ways of doing it," she said. "Have you tried being very affectionate?"

"Yes, indeed," said I.

"How did it answer?"

"He was bored to death."

"Have you tried being cool and distant? Being, so to speak, a stranger to him?"

"Yes, I have."

"And he?"

"He never even noticed that I was being a stranger to him. He was as happy and good-tempered as ever."

Olga shook her head dejectedly. "Have you tried being hysterical?" she asked after a while.

I hesitated. "I think so," I said at last. "But I do not quite know what you mean."

"Well," explained Olga sententiously, "with some men, who cannot bear healthy normal women, hysteria is a great success. Of course, it must be esthetic hysteria—you must try to preserve the plastic line through it all," and Olga sketched with her thumb a vague painter's gesture in the air. "For example, you deluge yourself in strange perfumes. You trail about the house in weird clinging gowns. You faint away at the sight of certain shades of color—"

"What an absurd idea!" I exclaimed.

"Not at all. Not in the least," said Olga. "On the contrary, it is very modern, very piquant to swoon away every time you see a certain shade of—of mauve, for instance."

"But what if I don't see it?"   '

"Silly! You *must* see it. Give orders to a shop to send you ten yards of mauve silk. Open the parcel in your husband's presence. Then—then you totter; you fall down—but mind," added Olga, "that you fall in a graceful, impressionist attitude. Like this." And Olga illustrated her meaning in what appeared to me a very foolish posture.

"I think it ridiculous," I said to her. And she was deeply offended.

"Good-by," she said, pinning her hat on briskly and spitefully.

"No, no! Don't go away. Do not desert me," I implored. "Try to suggest something else."

Olga was mollified. After reflecting a few moments she remarked.

"Have you tried being a ray of sunshine to him?"

I lost patience with her. "What do you mean by a 'ray of sunshine'? You seem to be swayed by stock phrases, such as one reads in novels."

This time Olga was not offended. She explained that in order to be a ray of sunshine in a man's life, one must appear before him gay, sparkling and radiant at all hours of the day.

"Always dress in the lightest of colors. Put a ribbon in your hair. When you hear his footsteps, run to meet him and throw your arms round his neck. When he goes out, toss a flower to him from the window. When he seems dull or silent, take your guitar and sing to him."

"You know I don't play the guitar," I said pettishly.

"That does not matter. What really counts is the singing. The atmosphere that surrounds him should be bright with unstudied gaiety. He ought to live, so to speak, in a whirlwind of sunshine!"

"Well, I will try," I sighed, without much conviction.

I did try.

I dressed in the lightest of colors and I pinned a ribbon in my hair. When I heard his footstep, I ran to meet him and threw my arms round his neck.

"What is the matter?" he asked. "And what on earth have you got on your head? You look like a barmaid."

To the best of my powers I was a whirlwind of sunshine; and as soon as I saw that he was dull

and silent (and this occurred almost immediately)
I said to myself that the moment was come for me
to sing to him.

I sat down at the piano. I have not much ear,
but a fine strong voice, even if not always quite
in tune.

At the second bar Vassili got up, took his hat
and left the house. I threw a flower to him from
the window.

He did not come back for three days.

VIII

WHEN I talked it over with Olga, she was very sympathetic.

"I know," she mused, "that these things sometimes succeed and sometimes do not. Men are not all alike." Then she added: "But there is one sure way of winning them back. It is an old method, but infallible."

"What is it?" I asked skeptically.

"By making them jealous. It is vulgar, it is *rococo*, it causes no end of trouble. But it is infallible."

We reviewed the names of all the men who could possibly be employed to arouse Vassili's jealousy. We could think of no one. I was surrounded by nothing but women.

"It is past belief," said Olga, surveying me from head to foot, "that there should be no one willing to—"

I shook my head moodily. "No one on earth."

Olga grasped my wrist. "Stay! I have an idea. We will get some one who is not on earth. Some one who is dead. It will be much simpler. I remember there was an idea of that kind in

an unsuccessful play I saw a year or two ago.
What we need is a dead man—recently dead, if
possible, and, if possible, young. If he has com-
mitted suicide, so much the better."

"What on earth do you want with a dead man?"
I asked, shuddering.

"Why! can't you see? We will say that he died
for your sake!" cried Olga, "that he killed himself on your account. We will have a telegram
sent to us by some one in Russia. We will get
them to telegraph to you: 'I die for your sake.
Am killing myself. Farewell!' "

"But who is to sign it?"

"Oh, somebody or other," said Olga vaguely.
"Or we could have it signed with an imaginary
name, if you prefer it. That would enable us to
dispense with the corpse."

"I most certainly prefer that," I remarked.
"But, frankly, I can't see—"

"What can't you see? Don't you see the effect
upon Vassili of the news that a man has killed
himself for your sake? Don't you see the new
irresistible attraction which you will then exercise
over him? Surely you know what strange subtle
charm emanates from the 'fatal woman'—the
woman whose lethal beauty—"

"Very well, very well," I said, slightly encouraged. "Let us have the telegram written and sent to me."

We spent the rest of the afternoon composing it.

Three days later Vassili entered the drawing-room where Olga and I were having tea; he held a telegram in his hand; his face was of a ghastly pallor.

"He's got it," whispered Olga hysterically, pinching my arm.

"Mura," said Vassili; "a horrible thing has happened. Horrible!" His white lips trembled as he uttered the incoherent words:

"Dead—he is dead—he has killed himself—"

He was unable to go on. His voice broke in a sob.

I sprang to my feet. "Who, Vassili? Who?"

Olga thought the moment had arrived for putting things in the proper light. She turned to me with a significant glance, and grasped my hand.

"Ah! It is the man who loved you!" she exclaimed. "And this—this is what you dreaded!"

"What! What!" shouted Vassili, clutching her arm and pushing her roughly aside. Then he turned upon me and seized me by the shoulder. "You—you knew of this? You dreaded this?"

I stood trembling, struck dumb with terror. I

could hear the futile and bewildered explanations of Olga:

"Why, surely," she was saying with an insensate smile, "it is a thing that might happen to anybody. It is not her fault if people love her to distraction."

But Vassili was crushing my wrist. "My brother—he loved you?" he gasped.

"*Your brother?* Your brother—little Peter?" I stammered.

"Yes, yes! Peter," shouted Vassili. "My brother! What have you to do with his death?"

"Nothing, nothing." I groaned. "I swear it —nothing!"

And Olga, realizing at last that she stood in the presence of a genuine tragedy and not of the jest we had plotted, darted forward and caught his arm.

"Vassili, you are mistaken. She knows nothing about it; nothing whatever. We had planned a joke to play on you, and we thought—" She pursued her agitated and incoherent explanations.

Vassili looked from one to the other of us, scanning our faces, hardly hearing what Olga was saying. Suddenly he seemed to understand, and loosening his hold on my arm he fell upon the couch and buried his face in his hands.

The telegram had dropped on the carpet. Olga picked it up and read it; then she handed it to me:

Peter hanged himself last night. Come at once.
                                            TARNOWSKY.

We left for Kieff the same evening. Throughout the entire journey Vassili never spoke. I sat mournful and silent opposite him and thought of my brother-in-law, Peter. Not of the pale youth, already corrupted by absinthe and women, whom we had left at Kieff a few months before, but of the child Peter, in his short velvet suit and lace collar, whom I had loved so dearly in the days of my girlhood—little Peter who used to run to meet me in the sun-splashed avenues of the Villa Tarnowsky, trotting up with his little bare legs and serious face, stopping to be kissed and then trotting hurriedly off again, the nape of his neck showing fair and plump beneath the upturned brim of his sailor-hat.

How well I remember that sailor-hat! The black ribbon round the crown bore, between two anchors, the word, *"Implacable";* and from under that fierce device the round and gentle countenance of little Peter gazed mildly out into the world.

Little Peter's legs were always cold. He was

brought up in English fashion, with short socks even in the depths of winter. From afar you could see little Peter's chilly bare legs, crimson against a background of snow. Sometimes, rubbing his knees, he would say to me: "I wish God had made me of fur, instead of—of leather, like this." And again he would remark: "I don't like being alive. Not that I want to die; but I wish I had never begun."

And now little Peter had finished. Little Peter lay solemn and magnificent in the *chambre ardente* where his dead ancestors had lain solemn and magnificent before him. "Implacable" indeed he lay, unmoved by the tears of his mother and father; his lofty brow was marble; his fair eyelashes lowered over his quenched and upturned eyes.

When I thought of him thus I felt afraid.

And it seemed strange to be afraid of little Peter.

IX

AFTER we had crossed the Russian frontier another thought—a thought that filled me with unspeakable happiness—put all others to flight: my child! I should see my child again! All our relations would certainly be assembled at the Tarnowskys' house, so I should find my parents and my little Tioka there too. The image of the living child soon displaced the tragic memory of the dead youth. As the train sped towards Kieff my fever of gladness and impatience increased. Yes, to-morrow would be poor Peter's funeral, but this very evening I should clasp little Tioka in my arms!

Raising my eyes, I saw that Vassili was looking at me with a scowl. "I have been watching you for some time," he said. "Heartless creature that you are, to laugh—to laugh in the face of death."

"I was thinking of Tioka," I stammered. Vassili did not reply. But in the depths of my heart joy sang and whispered like a hidden fountain.

Thus, inwardly rejoicing, did I enter the house of death and hasten to the dark-red room—the very scene of Peter's suicide—in which they had placed my baby's cradle; thus, while others mourned with prayers and tears in the gloomy death-chamber, I ran across the sun-filled garden holding my infant to my breast. I hid myself with him in the orchard and laughed and laughed aloud, as I kissed his starry eyes and his tiny, flower-like mouth.

But Death, the Black Visitor, had entered my life. Little Peter had shown him the way, had opened the door to him.

From that day forward the dread Intruder never forsook my threshold.

Death, lurking at my door in terrifying silence, stretched out his hand at intervals and clutched some one belonging to me. Generally it was with a swift gesture—a fell disease or a pistol-shot—that he struck down and flung into the darkness those I loved.

But towards me Death comes with a slower, more deliberate tread. For years, ever since the birth of my little daughter Tania,—my white rosebud born midst the snows of a dreary winter in Kieff—I have felt Death creeping towards me, slow, insidious, inexorable, holding in his hand a knot of serpents, each of which will fasten its poisoned fangs upon me. Disease, the venomous snake, will hide in my bosom and thrust its way through my veins. The heavy snake of Grief will coil round my heart and crush me in its spirals. Insanity will glide into my brain and nest there. Then—last but not least horrible—the little glass viper, the syringe of Pravaz, whose fang is a hollow needle, will draw me into the thraldom of its virulent grip. It will spurt its venom into my blood. The bland balm of coca, the milky juice of the poppy, will flow into my veins, soothing, assuaging, lulling me into sleep and forgetfulness —only to waken me in renewed agony of suffering to a renewed bite of the envenomed fang. For the only antidote to the poison of narcotics is the narcotic itself, the only alleviation to the tearing agony of the poison generated by morphia is morphia again. And so the fatal sequence swings on forever, in ever-widening circles of torment. . . .

X

From Alexis Bozevsky to Stepan Nebrasoff.

KIEFF, *Thursday.*

DEAR STEPAN, MY GOOD FRIEND,—

I am here in the house of your cousin, Dr. Stahl, who seems to have grown longer and leaner than ever. He is a mere shadow. It is here that your letter reaches me. You tell me to write to you about myself. To-day, the 15th of October, 1903, I am twenty-four years old. What gift will Destiny give me for my birthday? Love? Wealth? A hero's death?

Your cousin Stahl, in his cavernous voice that seems to come echoing up from underground, says that the gift of Destiny is precisely these four-and-twenty years of mine! Perhaps he is right. I feel them eddying in my blood like four-and-twenty cyclones.

The world is a whirlwind of youth.

Kaufmann this morning lent me his sorrel stallion—the finest horse in the Empire—and I had a gallop along the bastions. All the women looked at me. In a phaeton I saw the brazen and beautiful Princess Theodora, blonde and torrid as a Mexican landscape. She was resplendent in amethyst and heliotrope, her red locks flaming to the sun; no one but a princess would permit herself to display such a riot of violent colors.

Soon afterwards I saw Vera Voroklizkaja, reclining in her carriage, aloof and severe as a vestal virgin; her glossy black tresses parted over her brow enclosed the narrow oval of her face like soft black wings. Beside her sat little Miriam Grey, clothed in her youthfulness as in an armor of roses. The

58

beauty of all these women courses through my blood like sun and wine.

Upon my word life is an excellent institution.

And you—what are you doing?

Ever yours,

BOZEVSKY.

The next day.

STEPAN, STEPAN, STEPAN!—

I am in love! Madly, sublimely, tragically in love! This morning I went to the parade-ground as in a dream; I found myself speaking to the colonel in a gentle winning voice that was perfectly ludicrous. When I drilled my company I could hear myself giving the words of command in an imploring tone which I still blush to remember. I am obsessed, hallucinated; there floats before my eyes a slender, ethereal creature, with red lips that never smile, and hair that looks like a cataract of champagne.

Stahl introduced me to her yesterday, here at his house. "Come," he said, taking me by the arm. "You are going to make the acquaintance of a superior being, soft of voice and sad of countenance, who bears the gentle name of Marie."

"Let me off," I replied skeptically. "Sad and superior beings are not to my liking."

"You will like this one," said Stahl.

"I know I shan't." I replied curtly. I saw Stahl's eye warn me, and, turning, found myself face to face with the subject of our conversation, a tall, flower-like vision, with translucent eyes and a mystic inscrutable face.

I knew she had overheard me, and as I bowed low before her, she said: "That you should like me is of no importance. What really matters is that I should be pleased with you."

Her beauty and the scornful levity of her words struck me strangely. "Madame," and I was surprised to feel that I spoke with sincerity, "to please you will be henceforward the highest aim of my desire."

She looked at me a moment; then she spoke quietly: "You have attained your aim."

She turned and left me. I stood thunderstruck by the brief and daring reply and by the flash of that clear gaze. She had spoken the words without a smile.

She did not address me during the rest of the evening. When she left, she barely glanced at me and vouchsafed neither smile nor greeting.

Just for an instant she raised her black-fringed eyes and gazed at me; then her lashes fell; and it was as if a light had been blown out.

I am in love with her! Madly, divinely, desperately in love. Ah, Stepan, love—what an ecstasy and what a disaster!

Your Bozevsky.

It was Dr. Stahl, the "Satanic Stahl," who got these letters from his cousin Stepan Nebrasoff, and showed them to me. They bewildered and troubled me. What? ·Was I really so attractive and so perturbing in the eyes of the gallant young Pole—the handsomest officer in the Imperial Guard? I repeated to myself his disquieting epithets: "flower-like," "ethereal," "inscrutable"; and in my room at night when I loosened my hair, I wondered: "Does it really look like a cataract of champagne?" When I went out I never smiled, even when I felt inclined to do so, since my gravity had seemed so charming to him.

Night and day he followed me like a shadow—

or rather, should I say, like a blaze of light. In whatever direction I turned I was sure to encounter his radiant smile and his flashing glance. His passion encompassed me; I felt like Brunnhilde surrounded by a sea of flame. I was elated yet terrified.

One evening at dinner I made up my mind to speak to Vassili about it.

"Vassili," I said falteringly, "I think we ought to go away for a time."

"Away? Where to?" asked my husband.

"Anywhere—anywhere away from Kieff."

"Why?"

I felt myself turning pale! "I am afraid," I stammered, "I am afraid—that Bozevsky—"

"Well?" asked Vassili serenely, pouring some vodka into his champagne and drinking it.

"I am afraid that Bozevsky is falling in love with me."

"And who would not fall in love with you, dushka?" laughed Vassili. "As for Bozevsky, may the wolves eat him."

And dinner being over, he lit his cigar and went out.

.   .   .   .

I go sadly upstairs to the nursery where Tioka and Tania, like blonde seraphs, lie asleep.

A dim lamp hangs between the two white cots and illumines their favorite picture—an artless painting of the Virgin Mary, holding in her youthful arms the infant Jesus with a count's coronet on His head.

I kneel down beside the two little beds and weep.

Aunt Sonia, rectilinear and asexual in her gray flannel dressing-gown, comes in softly and bends over me.

"You must trust in Providence," she says, raising towards the ceiling her long virginal face. "And take a little camomile tea. That always does one good."

I obey her meekly and gratefully. It comforts me to think that a day will come when I also shall be like Aunt Sonia; when I also shall be content to wear gray flannel dressing-gowns and turn in my sorrows to Providence and to camomile tea.

And I wish that that day of peace were near.

XI

So we stayed on in Kieff and Bozevsky came
to see us every day. He brought me flowers—
wonderful orchids the color of amethyst, tenuous
contorted blossoms that looked as if they had
bloomed in some garden of dreams. He brought
me books; books of nebulous German poetry;
Spanish plays by Echegaray all heroism and fire;
and disquieting, neurotic French novels. Then he
brought me English books which filled me with
pleasant surprise. How far removed from our
Slav souls were those limpid Anglo-Saxon minds!
How child-like and simple was their wit, how
bland and practical their outlook on life. That
was the literature I liked best of all; perhaps because it was so different from everything in myself. I felt that I was a strange, ambiguous,
complicated creature compared with those candid
elemental natures.

Bozevsky liked to find me reading. He would
arrive in the evening—usually after Vassili had
gone out, alone or with friends—and enter

the drawing-room with bright and cheerful greeting. He always smiled when he found me with
one of his books in my hand, sitting beside Aunt
Sonia placidly knitting in her armchair.

"I like your thoughts to be far away from here,"
he would say, kissing my hand. "I like to know
that your soul is far from the frivolous society
you live in, far from the petty preoccupations,
the compliments and the flattery which surround
you. Let me read with you; let me join you
in the purer realm of fancy, far away from the
world." And he would sit down beside me, with
an air of protecting fraternal affection.

One evening he found me nervous and agitated.

"What has happened?" he asked.

"I have been reading a ghastly book," I told
him with a shudder. "The story of a mysterious
plant, a sort of huge octopus that feeds on human
flesh—"

"Ugh!" laughed Bozevsky, "how gruesome!"
and he bent his sunny head over the page.

"Just imagine," I continued, "its branches are
long moving tentacles, its thick leaves are quite
black and hard; they glitter and move like living
scorpions. . . ."

"Horrid, horrid," said Bozevsky with his shining smile as he took the book out of my hand.

"Forget the scorpions. To-night I shall read you some Italian poetry. I want you to make friends with Carducci."

He opened a plainly bound volume at random, and read to me.

"Oh favolosi prati d'Eliseo . . ."

I forgot the tree of scorpions. I forgot Bozevsky. I forgot Aunt Sonia and the world. The unknown poet had wrapped my spirit in his giant wings and was bearing me far away.

It was about this time that Vassili took me to Moscow. There, one evening, our friends the Maximoffs brought a stranger to see us. They introduced him as an estimable Moscow lawyer of high repute. I was surrounded by other friends and I greeted him absently, without hearing his name. I remember casually noticing that he was neither young nor old, neither ugly nor handsome. His wife, a timid, fair-haired woman, was with him.

At Vassili's suggestion we all went to the "Strelna," a famous night-restaurant. I remember that there was a great deal of laughter at the grotesque jokes which Vassili and Maximoff and also the estimable lawyer played on the pretty dark-faced tziganes.

I noticed that the lawyer's wife did not laugh. She passed her hand across her wistful Madonna-like brow, and listened only to the music.

Like her I felt out of tune with the merriment around me. My thoughts wandered back to the silent drawing-room at Kieff: I thought of Aunt Sonia and her peaceful knitting, of Bozevsky and the books he had brought me. I seemed to hear his voice saying, "Ugh! a tree of scorpions"— and at that very instant something cold and claw-like clutched my bare shoulder. I uttered a piercing shriek, which seemed to turn every one— including myself—cold with terror. But it was only the estimable lawyer, who, having drunk rather too much, had playfully climbed upon the sofa behind me and, to save himself from falling off, had laid his hand upon my shoulder.

"What on earth has happened?" exclaimed Vassili. "What made you scream like that?"

"I don't know," I stammered, taken aback, "I thought—I thought it was a scorpion!"

Every one laughed and for the rest of the evening the lawyer was nicknamed "the Scorpion." Perhaps this name added to the unreasoning fear I felt of him, or perhaps I was merely nervous, but he seemed to be always close behind me, and during the whole of that evening I kept on turning round, with little shivers running down my spine, to see what he was doing.

Suddenly he had disappeared. Vassili laughed loudly. "Hullo! Where 's the Scorpion?" And amidst the laughter of the guests he set himself to count the flippant tziganes one by one to see if any were missing. But they were all there— and I was glad for the sake of the Scorpion's poor little Madonna-wife.

It was three in the morning when we went back to our sleighs. It was very cold; the clear deep-blue sky was powdered with stars. Assisted by Maximoff I was about to step into the sleigh, when, with another cry, I drew back; my foot had touched something soft and shapeless that was lying huddled up beneath the rug.

"What is the matter now?" cried Vassili. "Another scorpion?"

No, it was the same one. It was the estimable lawyer very drunk and fast asleep at the bottom of the sleigh.

On our way back to the hotel, driving through the keen night air, I asked Vassili:

"Who was that man?"

"What man?" said Vassili, who sat opposite to us and was pressing the small feet of Maximoff's wife.

"You know—the man who frightened me."

"Oh, the Scorpion?" laughed Vassili. "That was Donat Prilukoff."

When we returned to Kieff I told Bozevsky the adventure of our evening at the Strelna, and described the Scorpion to him with as much humor as I could. But Bozevsky did not laugh. My absence had embittered and exasperated him. He no longer sat beside me with an air of protective fraternal affection. He would not speak of literature or poetry any more. He spent entire evenings making mute scenes of jealousy and despair, while dear Aunt Sonia, instinctively feeling the atmosphere around her charged with electricity, dropped many stitches in her knitting and became sour and irritable.

"My child, this must not go on any longer. Either Alexis Bozevsky must be forbidden the house or we ourselves must go away. I cannot understand how Vassili—" Her honest cheeks kindled with indignation. "Enough. I shall speak to him about it myself."

She did so: and Vassili, with his usual brief comment that we all bored him to death, expressed the hope that wild beasts might devour Bozevsky, and ordered us to pack up and leave for the country at once.

XII

So we all left for the country—to the great
delight of Aunt Sonia and the children.

Let my mind linger for an instant on those
springtide days—the last for me, though I did not
know it, of unalloyed serenity. The children and
I used to rise at dawn and go into the vast garden
all a-shimmer with dew. On the glittering lawn,
among the flower-beds, down the shady avenues
of the park the two little elfin figures flitted before
me, calling to me, eluding me, darting to and fro
like twin will-o'-the-wisps; then turned and ran
towards me with wind-light steps and gilt locks
afloat, to shelter in my outstretched arms. Oh!
my children, my little boy and girl, when you remember your mother I pray that God may lead
your memories back to those clear morning hours,
and may the rest be blotted out and dark.

Vassili was inexpressibly bored with rural solitude and sought new means of diversion. His
latest fad was target-shooting. He filled the
house with rifles and revolvers and invited every

one in the neighboring country houses to take part in shooting matches in our grounds. From morning to night, in the garden, in the courtyard, even from the windows of the house, there was a ceaseless crackling of firearms.

One afternoon when the house was filled with guests, Dr. Stahl and Bozevsky arrived in their troika from the neighboring castle of the Grigorievskys, where they had been staying. To my astonishment, Vassili received them jubilantly and embraced them both. He had quite forgotten the reasons which had led to our departure from Kieff.

Bozevsky came to greet me at once, and for the rest of the day never left my side. He enveloped me in a whirlwind of ecstatic tenderness. His infatuation, which he sought neither to conceal nor to control, disquieted me deeply.

I noticed that his friend Dr. Stahl watched us continually. I had not seen the doctor for many months, and he struck me as strangely altered. His very light eyes, in which the pupils were contracted until they seemed mere pin-points, followed me continuously.

"Doctor," I said to him, "what strange eyes you have! Just like the eyes of a cat when it looks at the sun!"

"I do not look at the sun," he answered slowly, speaking with great stress. "I look into an abyss, the abyss of annihilation and oblivion. Some day, if ever you are irremediably unhappy, come to me and I will open to you, also, the doors of my unearthly paradise—of this chasm of deadly joy which engulfs me."

"Shame on you, Stahl! How dare you suggest such a thing?" exclaimed Bozevsky, casting a look almost of hatred upon the morphinomaniac. "Why must you and your kind always seek to drag others down into your own gehenna?"

Stahl sighed. "It is terrible, I know. But it is a characteristic of our malady."

I listened without comprehending. I did not then know of Stahl's enslavement to the drug. "What are you speaking of? What malady? I do not understand."

"It is better not to understand," murmured Bozevsky with knitted brows. "Stahl is distraught; he is ill. Pay no attention to him. And never follow either his advice nor his example. But pray," he added, "do not worry your head over anything we have said; the shooting match will soon begin. I think your husband is looking for you."

But Vassili was far from troubling himself about

me. He was rushing to and fro setting up rows of bottles that were to serve as targets, and distributing guns and cartridges to all our guests. Then he hurried towards us. "There," he said to Dr. Stahl and to Bozevsky, giving them each a Flobert rifle, "these are for you."

"And what about the Countess?" asked Stahl in his hollow voice. "Is she not going to compete in the shooting?"

"Oh, no!" I exclaimed. "I am much too frightened."

"Nonsense!" cried Vassili, pushing a gun into my unwilling hands. "Of course you must shoot with the rest. And I warn you that if you are not brave I shall play William Tell with an apple on your head!" He passed on laughing, with Madame Grigorievskaja armed with a Browning by his side.

I was not at all brave; I held the rifle at arm's length, trembling with fear lest it should explode by itself. Stahl was amused by my terror, while Bozevsky sought to encourage and comfort me.

"Poor timid birdling," he murmured, "do not be frightened. See, I will teach you. It is done like this"—and he lifted the gun to my shoulder, placed my hands in position, and with his glowing face quite close to mine, showed me how I was to take aim. What with my terror of the gun and the fragrance of his fair hair near my cheek I felt quite dizzy.

"There, that's it. Now press the trigger."

"No! no! Don't say that! don't let me!" I screamed, incoherent with terror while Stahl and Bozevsky laughed.

Vassili from a distance caught sight of me: "Bravo, Mura!" he cried. "That's right. Go on. Shoot!"

"No! no!" I cried with my eyes shut and standing rigid in the position in which Bozevsky had placed me, for I dared not move a muscle.

Vassili called impatiently: "What on earth are you waiting for?"

Still motionless, I gasped:

"Perhaps—I might dare—if some one were to cover my ears."

Amidst great amusement Bozevsky came behind me and placed his two hands over my ears.

"Come now!" cried Stahl. "Do not be frightened."

"Mind you hit the third bottle," shouted Vassili from the distance.

Bozevsky standing behind me was clasping my head as though in a vice and whispering into my hair: "Darling, darling, darling! I love you."

"Don't," I cried, almost in tears under the stress of different emotions, "and don't hold my ears so tight."

The warm clasp relaxed at once.

"Oh, no, no!" I cried. "I can hear everything. I don't want to hear—," but even as I spoke the gun went off. I felt a blow near my shoulder, and thought I was wounded; but it was only the recoil of the weapon.

Everybody was laughing and applauding.

"What have I killed?" I asked, cautiously opening my eyes.

"The third bottle!" cried Vassili, and he was so delighted with my exploit that he ran up and embraced me. But the pistol he was holding in his hand and Bozevsky's glance of jealous wrath filled me afresh with twofold terror.

The afternoon passed as if in a dream. Vassili became very much excited and drank a great deal of vodka. Then Madame Grigorievskaja, who had once visited the United States, concocted strange American drinks which we had never tasted before—cocktails, mint-juleps, pousse-cafés and gin-slings. They were much approved of by every one.

I remember vaguely that half way through the afternoon some one let down my hair and set me among the shattered bottles with an apple on my head. I seem to see Vassili standing in front of me with a rifle and taking aim at me while the others utter cries of protest. Suddenly Bozevsky snatches the weapon from my husband's hands, and there is a brief struggle between them. Soon they are laughing again, and shaking hands—then Bozevsky joins me among the shattered bottles, and stands in front of me; he is so tall that I can see nothing but his broad shoulders and his fair hair. And Vassili is shooting—the bullets whirr over my head and all around me, but I have no sense of fear; Bozevsky stands before me, straight and motionless as a rampart.

We go in to dinner; gipsy musicians arrive and play for us. Late at night when the garden is quite dark we go out again to the targets; instead of the bottles Vassili has ordered a row of lighted candles to be set up, and we are to extinguish them with our shots without knocking them down. There is much noise around me; Vassili is dancing a tarantelle with Ivan Grigorievsky on the lawn. Dr. Stahl and Bozevsky are always by my side. I keep on shooting at the candles, but they spin round before my confused eyes like catharine-wheels; and Stahl laughs, and Bozevsky sighs, and the gipsies play. . . .

Suddenly Tioka's nurse comes hurriedly down the pathway towards me.

"May I speak to your ladyship for a moment?"

"Yes, Elise. What is it?"

"Master Tioka cannot go to sleep. He says you have forgotten to bid him good-night."

I put down my rifle and follow the straight small figure of Elise Perrier through the garden. I hasten after her into the house and upstairs to the nursery.

Little Tania is already fast asleep, with scarlet lips parted and silken hair scattered on her pillow. But Tioka is sitting up in his cot awaiting me. His bright soft eyes wander over my face, my hair, my dress; his innocent gaze seems to pierce me like a fiery sword. He holds out his arms to me and I hide my flushed face on his childish breast.

"Good-night, mother dear," he whispers, kissing me and patting my face with his small hand. Then he adds, with a funny little sniff at my cheeks and hair: "You smell of many things—of perfume and powder and cigarettes and wine . . ."

This sequence of gay words on the childish lips strikes at my heart like so many daggers.

"Hush, darling," I whisper, taking refuge in

those frail arms as in a haven of safety. "Forgive—forgive your mother."

But he does not know what there is to forgive; and he laughs and yawns and then nestles down in his pillow, still holding tightly to my hand.

"Must you go away?" he sighs, in a sleepy, endearing voice.

"No, darling, no. I will stay with you."

"Then tell me the poetry about the Virgin Mary coming down to see us in the night."

Holding my child's hand in my own, I begin softly:

> "When little children sleep, the Virgin Mary
> Steps with white feet upon the crescent moon . . ."

But already Tioka is in the land of dreams.

XIII

THE whole party of guests stayed at our house that night. Even one of the gipsy musicians was found next morning asleep on the sofa in the library.

No one came down to breakfast. Only Bozevsky got up early and went for a gallop on the hills.

I awoke at eight o'clock and rang the bell. Elise Perrier came in and opened the windows. The fresh April breeze blew in and the chirrup of the nests greeted me.

"Elise, is the morning fine? Can the mountains be seen?"

"Yes, my lady."

"Elise, when you see the mountains do you not feel homesick for Switzerland?"

"Yes, my lady." And Elise stooped down to set out my slippers and to hide the flush that rose to her face.

"I am homesick, too, Elise. I am homesick I hardly know for what—homesick for solitude and peace."

She made no reply.

"Should I find them in your Switzerland, do you think?"

Elise Perrier shakes her head and answers in a low tone: "No, my lady. Swiss homesickness and Russian homesickness are different."

"In what way?"

"We Swiss are homesick for—how shall I say? —for the outside things we are far away from . . . homesick for mountains and pine-trees and villages. But Russians are homesick for what they miss in their own hearts."

"You are right, Elise."

Tioka in his nightdress followed by Tania sucking the head of her favorite rubber doll have run gaily in and embrace me.

"Are we going to Switzerland?" cries Tioka, who has overheard what we were saying. "How nice! When do we start?"

"How nice! When do we start?" says Tania, who always echoes everything her brother says.

"I like to be always going away," adds Tioka.

And Tania repeats, "I like to be always going away."

I marvel at finding in these two children of mine, my own unrest already stirring, like a butterfly poised with quivering wings on the dawning flower of their souls.

I went down alone into the garden and entered the grove, where the sunshine only penetrates with mild rays of almost lunar whiteness. The grass under my feet was studded with periwinkles, their prim, pert faces lifted to the sky; tenuous ferns unfolded their embroidered scrolls, and masses of gentle wild violets, conscious of their pallor and their scentlessness, drooped shyly in the shade.

In the branches overhead wild hidden birds tried their new springtide voices in soft modulations and trills, or in long-drawn contralto notes of liquescent sweetness. Thus April spoke to me in gentle voices. With a sudden overwhelming longing to be nearer to the very soul of spring, I knelt on the grass and buried my face in the cool leaves and blossoms, bidding my heart be pure and cool as they.

On my homeward way I passed the targets. The servants had put everything in order—pistols, rifles and cartridges; and a fresh row of bottles seemed to await with glassy eye the shots of the amateur marksmen. With a deep sense of humiliation I remembered the feverish agitations of the previous day, and once more I said to myself: "Henceforward may my life be serene and pure."

A gay voice rang out close behind me, and startled me from my reverie.

"Lady Marie, good morrow!" It was Bozevsky, who, clicking his spurred heels together, saluted me with a radiant smile. His morning canter seemed to have given him an added touch of beauty and of daring; his fair hair gleamed in the sunshine, his smile was reckless and resplendent.

I bowed without speaking and attempted to pursue my way to the house, but he took my hand and detained me.

"Why go in? Everybody is still asleep. Come now," he urged, with a frank engaging smile, "stay here for awhile and practise at the targets."

So saying he chose a rifle and loaded it. Then he held it out to me. I took it from him and put it to my shoulder. I aimed carefully and was about to press the trigger when suddenly Bozevsky, with a lightning movement, put out his hand and pressed his palm against the muzzle of my gun.

"Wait!" he cried, with a wild, extravagant laugh. "Wait a moment! Before you press the trigger I want you to say—'Alexis, I love you!'"

"You are mad!" I exclaimed. "Take away your hand!"

"No. First you must say—'Alexis, I love you.'"

I felt a hot flush rise to my brow. "Take away your hand!" I repeated and looked steadily at him.

He did not move.

"Take it away, I implore you!"

Still he never moved, and I could see that hand stopping the muzzle of my gun—a long, slender hand with fingers separate and outstretched, and I felt almost as if I were under the influence of some hallucination. It was not only *his* hand that I saw—I seemed in a kind of frenzy to see the hands of all men outstretched before me, ready to grasp me, to crush me, to beat me down. Doubtless a wave of madness swept over me; a convulsive spasm shook my wrist—and the gun went off. I saw the long, lithe hand drop like some wounded creature.

With a cry I let the rifle fall, and covered my face. But Bozevsky had sprung upon me, and with his other hand seized both mine and pressed them down. He was as white as death. "You little tigress," he gasped. Then, as I was about to cry out again, he covered my mouth with his shattered hand, and I felt the blood gush over my face.

What distant heritage of madness broke upon us at that moment? What primitive frenzy lashed us together in a fierce embrace? I cannot tell. All I know is that from that hour I was his —tamed, vanquished, broken in spirit, and yet glad. He was the first, the last, the only lover of my devastated youth, and by his side the brief springtime of my happiness flowered and died. When the fearful death that was so soon to lay him low came upon him, when I saw him fall at my feet shot by Vassili—my reason gave way. The rest of my life lies behind me like a somber nightmare landscape, through which I wander, groping in the dark, stumbling forward on my way to perdition . . .

Yet sometimes I dream that it is all not true, that he still lives, that one day the door of my cell will open, and the lover of my youth appear to me again. I shall see him standing on the threshold, a halo of sunshine lighting his fair hair, like some young martyr-saint come to deliver me from my bondage. The hand I wounded will be filled with roses, and his clear voice will call me by my name.

Then rising from this gloomy prison bench I

shall move to meet him. Shame and crime and captivity will fall away from me like a dark and worn-out cloak.

Free and fair as in those distant April days in which he loved me, with white, winged footsteps I shall follow him.

XIV

Suddenly, almost from one day to another, Vassili grew jealous. When I had adored him he had neglected and forsaken me. Now that he feared to lose me he was inconsolable.

"You and Tioka are very much alike," I said to him one day when we were all at luncheon.

"Do you think so?" said Vassili, patting his little son's fair head and contemplating the small face, which at that moment was making a terrible grimace over its food. "What makes you say so?"

"You shall see." I leaned over to the child. "Tioka, my darling, won't you eat your nice dinner?"

"No!" said Tioka with great decision.

"Come, now, darling, eat your nice soup," and I held a spoonful to his lips.

"No," said Tioka, turning his face away.

"Why not, dear? Don't you like it?"

"No. It's nasty."

"Well, then," I said, putting down the spoon, "we will give it to the farmer's little boy."

"No! no!" cried Tioka, and he quickly devoured the soup in large spoonfuls.

Vassili laughed. "He is quite right. His soup is not for the farmer's little boy. To each one his own soup, is n't that so, Tioka?"

"No," said Tioka.

"Why 'no'? You should say 'yes.'"

"No," declared Tioka doggedly. "This is my 'no' day."

"Your *what?*" exclaimed his father.

"My day for saying 'no,'" announced Tioka with great decision.

His father was much amused. "I also shall have my 'no' days," he declared. "And I shall begin at once. To-day, Mura, we shall receive no visitors."

"But, Vassili," I protested, "we must see the Grigorievskys; we have invited them to dinner."

"No," said my husband.

"And Semenzoff. And Bozevsky."

"No," he repeated.

"Do you really mean that we are not to receive them?"

"No," he reiterated. "This is my 'no' day." And the reception for that evening was actually put off. The jest seemed highly entertaining to Vassili. I heard him laughing to himself as he

went downstairs; and in the days that followed
he frequently repeated it.

Shortly afterwards he took us all back to Kieff
and there he had many "no" days. In particular
he would not let Bozevsky visit us; and more than
a month passed without my seeing him.

At last it happened that the Stahls invited us
to a ball, and Vassili, who chanced to be in a good
temper, accepted. I knew I should meet Bozevsky there, and at the mere thought of seeing him
again I trembled with joy and fear.

Elise Perrier dressed me in a filmy gossamer
gown of soft opalescent tints, and fastened
round my neck the famous O'Rourke pearls—
those pearls which, according to family traditions,
had once decorated the slender neck of Mary
Stuart.

As Vassili put me into the troika he was all
kindness and amiability; he wrapped me closely
in the furs, and then took his seat beside me,
muffling himself up to his nose in the bearskins.
The horses started and we were off like the
wind.

During the drive tender and kindly feelings
towards Vassili filled my heart. I said to myself
that perhaps he was after all not wholly to
blame for his faults and follies. He, too, was

so young; perhaps if I had been less of a child
at the time of my marriage I should have known
how to make him love me more. And, after all,
were we not still in time to reshape our lives?
What if we were to go far away from Kieff, far
from St. Petersburg, and try to take up the thread
of our broken idyll again? My hand sought his.
He grasped it and held it warmly clasped under
the rug without turning towards me; I could
see his eyes shining under his fur cap as he gazed
straight before him, while we sped over the silent
snow. During that drive, from the bottom of
my heart, I forgave him all his transgressions
and silently craved forgiveness for mine. Already
I seemed to see myself with him and the children
and Aunt Sonia happily secluded in some smiling
rose-clad mansion in Italy. He would take up
the study of his music again, perhaps he would
compose, as he had often spoken of doing—while
I, seated at his feet, would read the Italian poets
that I loved, raising my eyes now and then to con-
template the motionless blue wave of the distant
Apennines . . .

But the troika had stopped, and Vassili sprang
out upon the snow. Through the illuminated
windows the tzigane music poured forth its waves
of sensuous melody—and alas! the rhythmic

swing of it swept away, as in a whirlwind, the peaceful dreams of Italy, of the rose-clad mansion and the Italian poets.

While the servants were taking our cloaks and snowshoes from us I whispered hurriedly to Vassili: "Dearest, be good to-night. Do not drink much."

"Why not? What a strange idea!" he said; and we passed into the overheated, overlighted rooms.

At the far end of the ballroom some thirty tziganes, women and men, in their picturesque costumes were making music. The men played and the women sang. The dancing couples whirled round in the scent-laden air.

Doctor Stahl's wife, a kindly German woman, received us with amiable smiles; Stahl himself greeted us with excited effusiveness. He was quite pale with two red spots on the summit of his cheeks. I was struck anew by his strange air of intoxication, for I knew he never touched wine. Immediately, from the end of the room Bozevsky came hastening to meet us, superb in his full uniform—blue tunic and scarlet belt.

"Hail *Fata Morgana!*" he cried. "Give me this dance," and he put his arm round my waist. But I drew back.

"Alas, Prince Charming, I dare not."

He turned pale; then he bowed, twirled on his heels and moved away. He did not come near me again until late in the evening. I saw him surrounded by women, who danced with him, smiling into his face, floating with languid grace in his arms.

I shrank into a corner of the vast room where tall plants and flowers screened me from the dancers.

"Why, what are you doing hidden here?" cried Stahl, coming up to me. His pupils were narrower than ever and his breath came and went in short gasps. He bent over me and scanned my face. "What are your thoughts, Countess Marie?"

"I have no thoughts," I replied sadly.

"Then I will give you one," said he laughing; "a blithe and comforting thought—think that a hundred years hence we shall all be dead!"

"True," I answered, and a wave of unspeakable melancholy invaded my soul. "We may, perhaps, be dead even fifty years hence."

"Or thirty," laughed Stahl.

"Or twenty," I sighed, in even deeper despondency.

"Oh, no," said Stahl. "Twenty years hence you will still be a charming matron getting on

towards middle-age." And, as some one was calling him, he turned away and left me.

His words sank into my heart, heavy and searing
as molten lead. How short, how short was life!
How the years flew past! How brief were the
wings of youth and happiness! I raised my eyes
—doubtless they were full of sadness—and I
saw that Bozevsky at the far end of the room
was looking at me. Several brilliantly attired
women were laughing and talking to him, but abruptly, without excuse or explanation, he left them
and crossed the room to where I sat.

The tziganes were playing a wild, nerve-thrill-
ing czarda. Without a word Bozevsky put his
arm round me and drew me into the dance.

The music went faster and faster, wilder and
ever more wild.

Light as air I swung round in Bozevsky's arm.
I could have wished to dance thus forever—dance,
dance to the very brink of life and, still dancing, to plunge over into the abyss of death.

As we whirled round I perceived that Vassili
was watching us. He was drinking champagne
with vodka in it and was laughing loudly while
he spoke to Stahl; but his eyes never left me as
I swept round the ballroom with Bozevsky. His
gaze alarmed me. I was dizzy and out of breath,

but I did not dare to stop dancing for fear of Vassili. I danced and danced, breathless and distraught; I felt my heart beating furiously, pulsing with the mad rapidity, the battering throb of a motor-cycle at full speed—and still I danced and danced on, while the ballroom, the guests, the tziganes spun round and round before my blurred eyes . . .

Vassili's gaze still followed me.

XV

Suddenly my strength failed me. The room seemed to be paved with water; the floor yielded and undulated under my feet; the motor-cycle pulsing in my breast stopped dead. Then I felt Bozevsky's arm sustain me as I fell forward on his breast. Everything whirled, darkened— vanished.

When I opened my eyes I was seated near the window; the dancers crowded round me. Stahl was bending over me with a small shining instrument in his hand. It was a hypodermic syringe.

I shrank back in terror. "No, no!" I cried.

Seeing that I had recovered my senses Vassili, who stood behind me, laid an iron hand on my bare shoulder.

"Come," he said in a hoarse and brutal voice. "Come at once."

"Where to?" I rose trembling to my feet. I still felt dizzy and weak, and scarcely knew where I was.

"Home," said Vassili, bending over me with a terrible look. His face was so close to mine that I could feel his breath upon me, hot and laden

93

with' that subtle sweetish exhalation of ether that vodka leaves behind it. "The dance is over," he muttered. "It is over, it is over." I noticed his clenched fists; and I was afraid. A deep silence had fallen on the entire room. "Come!" he repeated in a tone that made me quake.

I shrank back in terror. Then Vassili put out his hand and seized my pearl necklace; it broke in his grasp. The milky gems fell to the ground and rolled away in all directions; the guests, both men and women, stooped down to search for them and pick them up.

But now Bozevsky had taken a step forward, and stood, haughty and aggressive, in front of Vassili. He uttered a brief word in a low voice.

Vassili turned upon him with livid countenance. "Insolent scoundrel!" he cried, wildly searching his pockets for a weapon; then in a frenzy he turned on the awe-stricken assembly: "Go away, everybody!" he shouted. "Stahl, turn out the lights. We are going to have a game of blind man's buff, the Uhlan and I. A game of blind man's buff in the dark! Quick, Stahl, give us a couple of revolvers. Send all these people away and turn out the lights."

He was beside himself with vodka and with wrath.

Bozevsky still faced him, calm and unmoved. "Why should it be in the dark, Count Tarnowsky? Why not in the light of day—at ten paces?"

"No!" roared Vassili. "I 'll kill you in the dark, evil beast that you are. I 'll slaughter you like a wild beast in the dark!"

I never knew how we succeeded in getting him out into the troika, but at last the feat was accomplished, and he drove off with Madame Grigorievska and Semenzoff, the only two people who had any influence over him. I followed in another sleigh, alone with Dr. Stahl, who during the entire drive panted and shivered beside me, as if in the throes of some fierce physical agony.

Through the starry calm of the night, while the sleighs glided silently over the snow, we could hear Vassili's strident and drunken voice still roaring: "Blind man's buff with the officer! Ha, ha, ha! In the dark—bing bang. Blind man's buff!"

The scandal in Kieff was enormous. The whole town spoke of nothing else. All the women sided

with Vassili, and all the men with me. As for
Vassili, he cared nothing for the opinion of either.
He came and went with lowering brows, never
speaking either to me or to the children.

I was unspeakably frightened and unhappy.
At last, one evening, unable to endure the strain
of his silence any longer, and praying God to give
me courage, I went tremblingly and knocked at
his study door.

He said "Come in," and I entered.

He was standing by the window, smoking, and
he turned upon me a cold vindictive eye.

"Vassili"—my voice trembled—"Vassili, don't
be angry with me any more. Forgive me. I did
not mean to offend you. I did not mean—" I
burst into tears.

He seemed somewhat moved and held out his
hand to me without speaking.

I grasped it eagerly. He continued to smoke
and look out of the window, while I stood awk-
wardly beside him, holding his hand and not knowing what to say.

Perhaps my silence pleased him, for soon I felt
him press my trembling fingers more closely.
Looking timidly up into his face I saw that his
lips were quivering.

"Vassili," I whispered.

He turned to me abruptly. "Let us go away," he said, "Mura, let us go away!"

"Where?" I asked, overcome with sudden fear.

"Far away from here, far away from Russia. I cannot live in this accursed country any longer." And Vassili let go my hand in order to clench his fists.

"I had thought of it, too," I said unsteadily. And in a low voice I told him my thoughts of the rose-clad house in Italy, my dreams of an azure exile in that beauteous land, alone with him and the children.

"Mura! Mura!" he said, taking my face between his hands and gazing deeply into my eyes. "Tell me—is it not too late?"

Was it too late?

In my soul my unlawful passion for Bozevsky rose like a giant wave, towered over me, enveloped and submerged me. Then—then to the eyes of my spirit there came the vision of my children, of a flower-filled Italian garden, of peace reconquered and deliverance from evil. "No, Vassili, no. It is not too late!"

With a sigh I lay my cheek against his shoulder and bowed my face upon his breast.

Before our departure from Russia, in order not to leave ill-feeling or evil talk behind us, it was decided that Vassili and Bozevsky should meet and be reconciled.

The Stahls and Grigorievskys gladly undertook to organize an afternoon reception at which we were to take leave of all our friends and acquaintances. After that there would be a theater party at the opera, and, finally, the more intimate of our friends were to be the guests of Bozevsky himself at a supper at the Grand Hotel. There we were to say farewell to one another for many years, perhaps forever.

In spite of the burning desire which drew me towards Bozevsky, I had honorably kept my part of the agreement and had refused to see him for even an instant before the appointed day.

Vassili took the necessary steps to get our passports and every preparation was made for our final departure from Russia.

And now the eve of our journey had come—the afternoon reception was over; and this was the fatal evening which was to mark the supreme and ultimate hour of my happiness.

Satins and jewels decked my aching heart; flowers garlanded my ringleted hair; I wanted Alexis to see me for the last time looking my fairest. I longed to remain forever in his memory a loved and radiant vision.

"You are dazzlingly beautiful," said my cousin Vera to me, as soon as I entered the room, surveying me from top to toe. "I can quite understand why every one is crazy about you."

I was immediately surrounded by all our most intimate friends, who lamented in every key our resolve to leave Russia.

"Without you, Kieff will be empty. It will be like a ring which has lost its brightest gem."

I smiled and sighed, feeling both gratified and mournful.

Who would have thought that after this evening all those who now surrounded me with flattering words would pass me by without a greeting, would turn from me as from some vile and tainted creature?

Bozevsky, pallid and stern, came to me, and bowed low as he kissed my hand.

"*Ave! Ave . . . Maria!*" he said. Then he raised his eyes and looked at me long and fixedly. Despair was so clearly written on his countenance, that I felt afraid lest Vassili should notice it; Alexis read the fear in my eyes, and laughed. "Do you know what I believe?" he said.

I looked at him without understanding.

"I believe," he continued in scornful tones, "that I am in a trap."

"A trap? What do you mean?" I gazed questioningly into his face.

"Yes, yes, a trap," said he with a cynical laugh. Then in a tone that seemed in keeping with the frivolous atmosphere that surrounded us:

"Countess," he continued, "has it ever happened to you to go wrong in some well-known quotation? To begin, for instance, with one author, and to end with another?"

"I do not understand," I stammered, perplexed by the strangeness of his manner. "What—what do you mean?"

Vassili was approaching, and Alexis with a scornful laugh raised his voice slightly as he spoke. "Because to-night," he said, "a misquotation of that kind keeps ringing through my brain. *"Ave, Maria! . . . Morituri te salutant!"*

Vassili stood beside us and heard the words with a puzzled smile.

"Morituri?" he said, holding out his hand to Bozevsky with a frank and friendly gesture. *"Morituri?* Indeed I hope not."

Bozevsky took his hand and looked him in the face. Vassili returned his gaze; then, with an impulsive gesture, in true Russian fashion, my husband bent forward and kissed him on both cheeks.

No! no, it was not a trap! From the depths
of my broken heart, from my inmost consciousness, there springs up this protest on behalf of
him who on that fatal evening wrecked my life.
I know that it was an impulse of his fervent heart
that impelled Vassili to open his arms to the man
whom an hour before he had hated—and whom an
hour later he slew.

No; it was not a trap.

XVI

Doubtless that evening I was beautiful. During the supper party at the Grand Hotel I felt that I diffused around me an atmosphere of more subtle intoxication than the music or the wines. Placed between Vassili and Stahl I laughed and laughed in a fever of rapturous gaiety. I was excited and overwrought.

Bozevsky sat facing me. As I glanced at his proud, passionate face, I said in my heart: "To-morrow you will see him no more. But this evening he is here; you see him, pale for the love of you, thrilled by your presence. Do not think of to-morrow. To-morrow is far away!"

So I laughed and laughed while the rhythmic charm of waltzes played on muted strings wrought upon my senses, swaying me towards an unreal world, a world of transcendent passion and incomparable joys.

Stahl, seated at my right hand, was flushed and elated, but still drew the hurried sibilant breaths I had so often noticed in him. Vassili seemed to have fallen in love with me anew. He murmured rapturous words into my ear. "To-morrow you shall be mine, mine only, out of reach of all others, beyond the sight and the desire of all these people —whose necks I should like to wring." And he drank his Clicquot looking at me with kindling eyes.

"Vassili," I whispered imploringly, "do not drink any more."

"Don't you wish me to?" he asked, turning to me with his glass of champagne in his hand. "Don't you wish it? Well—there!" He flung the glass full of blonde wine behind him over his shoulder. The thin crystal chalice was shattered into a thousand pieces.

"What are you doing, Vassili? What are you doing?" cried Grigorievsky. "Are you playing the King of Thule?"

"Precisely," laughed Vassili. "Was he not the paragon of all lovers, who chose to die of thirst in order to follow his adored one to the grave?"

And somewhat uncertainly he quoted:

> "Then did he fling his chalice
> Into the surging main,
> He watched it sink and vanish—
> And never drank again."

"Here's to the King of Thule!" cried one of the guests. And they all drank Vassili's health.

Bozevsky had sprung to his feet; his eyes gleamed strangely. "You may be the King of Thule, Tarnowsky," he cried in a mocking tone, "but I am the knight Olaf. You know the legend?" His clear insolent eyes surveyed the guests provocatively. "Olaf—you remember—was condemned to death for daring to love the king's daughter. He was at his last banquet. 'Take heed, Olaf,' said the king. 'The headsman stands at the door!' 'Let him stay there, sire, while I bid farewell to life in a last toast!' And standing up—just as I stand here—he raised his glass, as I raise mine:

> "I drink to the earth, I drink to the sky,
>   I drink to the sea and the shore;
> I drink to the days that I have seen,
>   And the days I shall see no more;
> I drink to the King who has sentenced me,
>   And the Headsman at the door.
>
> "I bless the joys that I have had
>   And the joys that I have missed;
> I bless the eyes that have smiled on me
>   And the lips that I have kissed!"

Here Bozevsky turned and looked straight at me:

> "To *thy* red lips that I have kissed
>   I raise this cup of wine,

> I bless thy radiant loveliness
> That made my life divine,
> And I bless the hour that brings me death
> For the hour that thou wert mine!"

He uttered these words in a loud voice, with his daring eyes fixed steadily on mine; then he raised his glass and drained it.

Vassili had sprung to his feet. But instantly Stahl was beside him, speaking rapidly, while Grigorievsky exclaimed:

"The sleighs are waiting. It is time to go home!"

Amid nervous and hurried farewells the perilous moment passed and the danger was averted. We all hastened to our sleighs; my cousin Vera and Madame Grigorievska were beside me; Stahl and Grigorievsky had each with an air of easy friendliness taken my husband by the arm.

"Good-by! Good-by! *Bon voyage!* Good-by!" The last farewells had been exchanged. The impatient horses were shaking their bells in the icy night air. Vera had already taken her place in the sleigh, and I was about to step in beside her, when I saw Bozevsky striding rapidly towards me. He passed in front of my husband, who was standing near the second sleigh with Stahl and Grigorievsky, and came straight to me.

He stretched out his hand with a gesture of despair.

"So it is all over—all over!" he said. "And this is good-by!"

His voice broke, and he bent his fair head over my hand, crushing my fingers in his feverish clasp.

At that instant the report of a shot rang out, followed by a mad outburst of laughter from Vassili. I saw the horses of the sleigh plunge and rear.

Bozevsky, still clasping my hand, wrenched himself upright; a convulsive shiver passed through him, and his head jerked backwards with a strange, wooden movement like that of a broken doll—then with a shrill burst of laughter which showed all his teeth, he fell forward at my feet.

With a cry I bent over him, and I felt a splash of blood on my face. It spurted forth like the jet of a fountain from the side of his neck. Once again my hands, my dress were covered with his blood—I thought I was in a dream. Every one had come rushing up. Now they raised him. I saw Stahl snatch a white scarf from some one's shoulders and wind it round and round the wounded neck, and immediately a dark stain appeared on the scarf and slowly widened.

Supported by Stahl, Bozevsky stared about him with haggard eyes, until his gaze met mine.

A quiver passed over his face. "I bless the hour—" he gasped. Then a gush of blood came from his mouth, and he was silent.

XVII

Bozevsky was carried to his room and the manager and servants of the Grand Hotel thronged in murmuring consternation round his door. A Swedish doctor, staying at the hotel, was summoned in haste. He appeared in his dressing-gown, and with Stahl's assistance carefully dressed and bound up the deep double wound caused by the bullet, which had passed through the left side of Bozevsky's neck and come out beneath his chin.

Trembling and weeping I followed the sinister procession, and with Cousin Vera and Madame Stahl entered Bozevsky's room. Now I stood, silently praying, at the foot of the bed. Bozevsky sunken in his pillow, with his eyes closed and his head and neck in bandages, looked as if he were already dead.

He suddenly opened his eyes, and his gaze wandered slowly from side to side until it rested on me. He moved his lips as if to speak, and I hastened to his pillow and bent over him.

He whispered, "Stay here."

"Yes," I said, and sat down beside him, taking his moist, chill hand between my own.

He repeated weakly: "Stay here. Do not go away."

The Swedish doctor was washing his hands and talking in a low voice to Stahl. He turned to me and said:

"You must try not to agitate him. Do not let him speak or move his head." Then he went out into the corridor with Stahl.

Mrs. Stahl and Vera sat mute and terror-stricken in a corner. I watched Bozevsky, with a deep, dull ache racking my heart. He seemed to be falling asleep. I felt his hand relax in mine and his short breathing became calmer and more regular.

But Stahl came in again, and Bozevsky opened his eyes.

Stahl approached the bedside and stood for a long while looking down at his friend. Then he turned to me. "A nurse is coming," he said. "I will take you ladies home and then come back and pass the night with him."

Take me home! How could I return home? How could I endure to meet Vassili again? At the mere thought of seeing him, who with a treacherous shot from behind had shattered this young existence, hatred and terror flamed up within me. No! I would not return home. Never again would I touch the hand of Vassili Tarnowsky.

While these thoughts traversed my mind, some one knocked at the door. It was the nurse. Vera and Madame Grigorievska, after questioning me with their eyes, got up softly; then, with a glance of pity at Bozevsky, they went on tiptoe out of the room.

At the door Stahl beckoned to me to come. But I shook my head. As if he knew what was passing Bozevsky opened his eyes again.

"Stay here," he whispered. Then he put his hand to the bandage round his neck. "If you leave me I will tear it all off." He made a gesture as if he would do so.

"I shall not leave you," I whispered bending over him. "I shall never leave you again."

I kept my word.

Later I learned that Vassili had given himself up to the authorities, and that my grief-stricken mother had come to fetch our children and had taken them with her to Otrada. To her and to my father they were the source of much melancholy joy.

Thus did the old garden of my youth open again its shadowy pathways and flowery lawns to the unconscious but already sorrow-touched childhood of little Tioka and Tania—those tragic children whose father was in prison and whose mother, far away from them, watched and suffered by the sinister death-bed of a stranger. To me the two innocent, angelic figures often came in my dreams; and I cried out to them with bitterest tears: "Oh, my own children, my two loved ones, forgive your mother that she does not forsake one who is dying for her sake. This very night, perhaps, or to-morrow—soon, soon, alas!—his life will end. And with a broken heart your mother will return to you."

But Bozevsky did not die that night. Nor the following day. Nor the day after.

Fate had in store for him and for me a much more appalling doom. He dragged his frightful death-agony through the interminable hours of a hundred days and a hundred nights. He was doomed to trail his torment from town to town, from surgeon to surgeon, from specialist to charlatan. One after another, they would unbandage the white and withered neck, probe the blue-edged wound, and then cover up again with yellow gauze the horrifying cavity; leaving us to return, heart-stricken and silent, to the luxurious hotels that housed our irremediable despair.

About that time I heard that Vassili had been released on bail. Later on he was acquitted by a jury in the distant city of Homel, on the ground of justifiable homicide.

Perhaps it was a just verdict. But for him whom he had struck down—and for me—what anguish, great Heavens! What lingering torture of heart-breaking days and nights.

Ah, those nights, those appalling nights! We dreaded them as one dreads some monstrous wild beast, lurking in wait to devour us. All day long we thought only of the night. As soon as twilight drew near Bozevsky, lying in his bed with his face towards the window, clutched my hand and would not let it go.

"I am afraid," he would murmur. "I wish it were not night. If only it were not night!"

"Nonsense, dearest," I would say, cheerfully. "It is quite early. It is still broad daylight. Everybody is moving about. The whole world is awake and out of doors."

But night, furtive and grim, crouched in the shadowy room, lurked in dark corners, and, then suddenly was upon us, black, silent, terrifying.

Round us the world lay asleep, and we two were awake and alone with our terror.

Then began the never-ending question, ceaselessly repeated, reiterated throughout the entire night:

"What is the time?"

It was only nine o'clock. It was half-past nine. . . . Ten . . . Half-past ten . . . A quarter to eleven . . . Eleven o'clock . . . Five minutes past . . .

As soon as it was dawn, at about four o'clock, Bozevsky grew calm. Silence fell, and he slept.

The last station of our calvary was at Yalta, in the Crimea. We had gone there with a last up-flaming of hope. There were doctors there whom we had not yet consulted. There was Ivanoff and the world-famed Bobros.

"Continue the same treatment," said the one.

"You must try never to move your head," said the other.

That was all.

And to our other tortures was added the martyrdom of complete immobility.

"I want to turn my head," Bozevsky would say in the night.

"No, dearest, no. I implore you—"

"I must. I must turn it from one side to the other. If I stay like this any longer I shall go mad!"

Then, with infinite precautions, with eyes staring and terror-filled, like one who yields to an overwhelming temptation or performs some deed of insane daring, Bozevsky would turn his sad face slowly round, and let his cheek sink into the pillow.

His fair curls encircled with flaxen gaiety his spent and desolate face.

XVIII

ALONE with him during those long terrible hours, my anguish and my terror constantly increased. At last I could endure it no longer and I telegraphed to Stahl:

"Come immediately."

At dusk the following day Stahl arrived.

I had hoped to derive courage and consolation from his presence. But as soon as he stepped upon the threshold my heart turned faint within me. Thinner and more spectral than ever, with hair dishevelled and eyes sunken and dull, he looked dreamily at me, while a continual tremor shook his hands.

I greeted him timorously, and the touch of his chill, flaccid fingers made me shudder.

Bozevsky seemed glad to see him. Stretching out his wasted hand to him he said at once:

"Stahl, I want to move my head."

Stahl seemed not to understand, and Bozevsky repeated: "I want to turn my head from one side to another."

"Why not?" said Stahl, sitting down beside the bed and lighting a cigarette. "Turn it by all means."

It was growing late; outside it was already dark. I drew the curtains and turned on the lights. Bozevsky began very slowly to turn his head from side to side; at first very timorously with frightened eyes, then by degrees more daringly, from right to left and from left to right.

"Keep still, keep still, dearest," I entreated, bending over him.

"Stahl said it would not hurt," panted Bozevsky. "Did you not, Stahl?" Stahl made no reply. He was smoking, with his heavy eyes half closed. At the sight of him I was filled with loathing and fear.

"Have you dined?" I inquired of him after a long silence. He nodded and went on smoking.

I tried to coax Bozevsky to take an egg beaten up in milk, but he continued to turn his head from side to side and would touch nothing. Little by little the sounds in the hotel died away. The gipsy music which had been audible, faintly in the distance, ceased. Night crept upon us sinister and silent.

Presently Stahl roused himself and opened his eyes. He looked at me and then at Bozevsky, who lay in the circular shadow cast by the lamp shade, dozing with his mouth slightly open; he looked pitiful and grotesque in his collar of yellow gauze.

Stahl made a grimace; then his breath became short and hurried as on that night of the ball when he sat beside me in the sleigh. He was panting with a slight sibilant sound and with a quick nervous movement of his head.

"Stahl," I whispered, leaning towards him and indicating Bozevsky, "tell me—how do you think he is?"

Stahl did not answer. He seemed not to have heard me, but to be absorbed in some mysterious physical suffering of his own.

"What is the matter, Stahl? What is the matter? You are frightening me."

With a nervous twist of his lips intended for a smile Stahl got up and began to walk up and down the room. His breath was still short and hurried. He drew the air through his teeth like one who is enduring spasms of pain.

Then he began to talk to himself in a low voice. "I can wait," he said under his breath. "I can wait a little longer. Yes—yes—yes, I can wait a little longer."

Bozevsky had opened his eyes and was watching him.

Horror held me motionless and shivers ran like icy water down my spine.

"Stahl, Stahl, what is the matter?" I said, and began to cry.

Stahl seemed not to hear me. He continued to walk up and down muttering to himself: "I can wait, I can wait. Just a little longer—a little longer—"

Bozevsky groaned. "Tell him to keep still," he said, his gaze indicating Stahl.

I seized Stahl by the arm. "You must keep quiet," I said. "Keep quiet at once."

He turned to me a vacuous, bewildered face. I grasped his arm convulsively, clutching it with all my strength: "Keep still!"

Stahl sat down. "Right," he said. "All right."

He searched his pocket and drew out a small leather case.

Bozevsky moved and moaned. "I am thirsty," he said. "Give me something to drink."

I hurried to the bedside, and taking up a glass of sweetened water, I raised him on his pillow and held the glass to his lips. He drank eagerly. Then—horror! . . . horror! Even as he drank I perceived a spot of pale red color, wetting the gauze round his neck, oozing through it and

spreading in an ever-widening stain. What—
what could it be? It was the water he was drinking; he was not swallowing it . . . it was trickling
out through the wound in his neck. All the gauze
was already wet—now the pillow as well.

"Stahl, Stahl!" I shrieked. "Look, look at
this!"

Stahl, who seemed to have suddenly regained
his senses, came quickly to the bedside. I had laid
Bozevsky back on the pillow and he was looking
at us with wide-open eyes.

"Yes," said Stahl, contemplating him thoughtfully. "Yes." Suddenly he turned to me.
"Come here, come here. Why should I let you
suffer?"

Then I saw that he had in his hand a small glass
instrument—a morphia syringe. He seized my
wrist as in a vice and with the other hand pushed
back the loose sleeve of my gown.

"What are you going to do?" I gasped.

"Why, why should you suffer?" cried Stahl,
holding me tightly by the arm.

"Are you killing me?" I cried.

"No, no. I shall not kill you. You will see."

I let him take my arm and he pricked it with
the needle of the syringe, afterwards pressing and
rubbing the punctured spot with his finger.

"Now you will see, now you will see," he repeated over and over again with a vague stupefied smile. "Sit down there," and he impelled me towards an armchair.

Bozevsky in his wet bandages on his wet pillow was watching us. I wanted to go to his assistance, to speak to him—but already a vague torpor was stealing over me, a feeling of gentle langour weighed upon my limbs. My tense and quivering nerves gradually relaxed. I felt as if I were submerged in a vague fluid serenity. Every anxious thought dissolved in a bland and blissful somnolence. . . . I could see Bozevsky move restlessly and again begin to turn his head from side to side. Sunk in the divine lassitude that held me, I watched his movements, glad that the sight of them gave me no pain.

I saw that Stahl had stretched himself on the couch and lay there with a vacant ecstatic smile on his lips.

All at once Bozevsky uttered a cry. I heard him, but I felt no inclination to answer. He struggled into a sitting position and looked at us both with wide, horrified eyes. He called us again and again. Then he began to weep. I could hear his weeping, but the beatific lethargy which engulfed me held me motionless. Perhaps I was even smiling, so free and so remote did I feel from all distress and suffering.

And now I saw Bozevsky with teeth clenched and hands curved like talons, madly clutching and tearing away the bandages from his neck.

He dragged and tore the gauze with quick frenzied movements, while from his lips came a succession of whimpering cries as of a dog imprisoned behind a door.

I smiled, I know I smiled, as I gazed at him from my armchair.

Stahl's eyes were shut; he was fast asleep.

Even when the wasted neck was stripped bare, those quick, frenzied movements still continued. What my eyes then saw I can never tell. . . .

Thus died Alexis Bozevsky, the handsomest officer in the Imperial Guard.

XIX

AFTER that all is dark. A blood-red abyss seems to open in my memory wherein everything is submerged—even my reason.

My reason! I have felt it totter and fall, like something detached and apart from myself; and I know that it has sunk into the grave that covers Alexis Bozevsky.

Vaguely, from my distant childhood, a memory rises up and confronts me.

I am in a school. I know not where. It is sunset, and I am at play, happy and alone, in the midst of a lawn; the daisies in the grass are already closed and rose-tipped, blushing in their sleep. Some one calls my name, and raising my eyes I see the small eager face of my playmate Tatiana peering out of an oval window in an old turret, where none of us are ever allowed to go. "Mura! Mura! Come quickly," she cries. "The turret is full of swallows!"

"Full of swallows!" I can still recall the ecstasy of joy with which those three words filled

me. I ran to the entrance of the old tower and
helter-skeltered up the dark and narrow staircase;
then, pushing aside a mildewed door, I found
myself with Tatiana in a gloomy loft, and yes, yes!
it was full of swallows!

They flew hither and thither, darting over our
heads, brushing our faces, making us shriek with
delight. We managed to catch any number of
them. Many were even lying on the ground.
Tatiana filled her apron with the fluttering creatures, while I held some in my handkerchief and
some in my hands. Then we ran downstairs into
the dining-hall: ''Look, look! we have caught a
lot of swallows!'' I can still see the girls crowd-
ing round us, and the face of the mistress bending
forward with an incredulous smile; I see her
shrink back, horrified and pale, with a cry of dis-
gust: ''Mercy upon us! They are all bats!''

Even now the recollection of the shrieks we uttered as we flung them from us makes my flesh
creep; even now I seem to feel the slippery smooth-
ness of those cold membranes gliding through my
fingers and near my cheeks. . . .

To what end does this childish recollection enter
into the dark tragedy of my life? This—that
when I mount into the closed turret of my mind
in quest of winged thoughts and soaring fancies,

alas! there glide through my brain only the monstrous spirits of madness, the black bats of hypochandria. . . .

I remember little or nothing of those somber days in Yalta. I can vaguely recollect Stahl telling me over and over again in answer to my delirious cries for Bozevsky: "He is dead! He is dead! He is dead!" And as I could not and would not believe him, he took me in a closed carriage through many streets; then into a low building and through echoing stone passages into a large bare room—a dissecting room!

The horror of it seals my lips.

Still more vaguely do I recollect the death of Stahl himself. I know that one evening he shot himself through the heart, and was carried to the hospital. I know that he sent me the following words traced in tremulous handwriting on a torn piece of paper: "Mura! I have only half an hour to live. Come to me, I implore you. Come!"

I did not go to him. The terrible lessons he had taught me were bearing fruit; all I did when brought face to face with some new calamity was to take injection after injection of morphia; and thus I sank down again into the twilight world of unreality in which, during that entire period, I moved like one in a dream.

I seemed to be living under water, in a perpetual dimness—a fluid, undulating dusk.

No sooner did I find myself rising to the surface of consciousness, and the noisy harshness of life confronted me again, than my trembling hands sought the case that hid the little glass viper of oblivion—the hypodermic syringe of Pravaz.

Over the tremulous flame of a candle I heated the phial of whitish powder and watched it gradually dissolve into a clear crystalline liquid that the hollow needle thirstily drank up: then I bared my arm and thrust the steel point aslant into my flesh. Soothing and benumbing the morphia coursed through my veins; and I sank once more into the well-known beatific lethargy, the undulating dusk of unreality and sleep. . . .

But one day a call thrilled through the enveloping cloud and reached my heart: it was the call of motherhood. Tioka! Tania! Where were my children? Why, why were my arms empty when these two helpless and beloved creatures were mine?

Horrified at myself and at the dream-like apathy in which I had strayed so long, I tore myself from the degrading captivity of narcotics and with trembling steps tottered towards the threshold of life once more.

With dazed eyes I beheld the altered world around me.

How everything had changed! I was no longer the Countess Tarnowska, flattered, envied and beloved. The women who had formerly been my friends turned their eyes away from me, while on the other hand men stared at me boldly in a way they had never dared to look at me before. Vassili—the frivolous, light-hearted Vassili—shut his door upon me, and secluded himself in grim and formidable silence as in the walls of a fortress. Vainly did I beat upon it with weak hands, vainly did I pray for pity. Inexorable and inaccessible he remained, locked in his scorn and his resentment. Nor ever have the gates of his home or of his heart opened to me again.

I took refuge with my children at Otrada.

My parents received us in sorrow and humiliation. Themselves too broken in spirit to offer me any consolation, they moved silently through the stately mansion, blushing for me before the servants, hiding me from the eyes of their friends.

Even my children hung their heads and crept about on tiptoe, mute and abashed without knowing why.

One day Tania, my little Tania, was snatched

from my arms. Vassili took her from me, nor did I ever see her again.

I had gone out, I remember, sad and alone, into the wintry park. By my side trotted Bear, my father's faithful setter, who every now and then thrust his moist and affectionate nose into my hand. In my thoughts I was trying to face what the future might have in store for me.

"When my little Tioka grows up," I said to myself, "I know, alas! that I shall lose him. He will want to live with his father: he will look forward to entering upon life under happy and propitious auspices. Yes, Tioka will leave me, I know. But my little girl will stay with me. Tania will be my very own. She will grow up, fair and gentle, by my side; I shall forget my sorrows in her clinging love; I shall live my life over again in hers. I shall be renewed, in strength and purity, in my daughter's stainless youth."

As I thus reflected I saw my mother running to meet me, her gray head bare in the icy wind; she was weeping bitterly. Tania was gone! Vassili had taken her away!

Notwithstanding all my tears and prayers it was never vouchsafed to me to see my little girl again.

But when the day came in which they sought to tear my son from me as well, I fought like a maddened creature, vowing that no human power should take him from me while I lived. I fled with him from Otrada—I fled I knew not and cared not whither, clasping in my arms my tender fair-haired prey, watching over him in terror, guarding him with fervent prayers. I fled, hunted onward by the restlessness that was in my own blood, pursued by the bats of madness in my brain.

Thus began my aimless wanderings that were to lead me so far astray.

Alone with little Tioka and the humble Elise Perrier, I took to the highways of the world.

How helpless and terrified we were, all three of us! It was like living in a melancholy fairy tale; it was like the story of the babes lost in the wood. Sometimes, in the midst of a street in some great unknown city, little Tioka would stop and say: "Mother, let us find some one who knows us, and ask them where we are to go and what we are to do."

"No, no! Nobody must know us, Tioka."

Then Tioka would begin to cry. "I feel as if we were lost, as if we were lost! . . ." And I knew not how to comfort him.

One day—we were at Moscow, I remember—there appeared to me for the first time that lean and threatening wolf which is called—*Poverty.*

Poverty! I had never seen it at close range before. I almost thought it did not really exist. I
knew, to be sure, that there were people in the
world who were in need of money; but those were
the people whom we gave charity to; that was all.

Poverty? What had poverty to do with us?

During all my life I had never given a thought
to money.

XX

"ELISE, I cannot bear to see myself in this ugly black dress any longer. Write to Schanz and tell him to send me some new gowns. I want a dark green tailor-made costume, and a pearl-gray voile."

"Yes, my lady. But, begging your ladyship's pardon, Schanz says that he would like to be paid."

"Well, let us pay him then."

"Yes, my lady. But, begging your ladyship's pardon, his bill is twenty-five thousand rubles."

"Well, let him have them."

"I am sorry, my lady, but we have not got twenty-five thousand rubles."

It was true. We had not got twenty-five thousand rubles.

"Elise, Tioka wants to be amused. He would like a toy railway."

"Yes, my lady."

"Mind," cried Tioka, "it must be like the one we saw yesterday, with all those stations and canals, and a Brooklyn bridge."

"Yes, Master Tioka."

"Well, Elise, what are you waiting for?"

"Begging your ladyship's pardon, it costs eighty rubles."

"Well?"

"We have not got them."

True enough; we had not got eighty rubles.

"Elise, I have no more perfumes. Go and get me a bottle of Coty's Origant."

"Yes, my lady. But—"

"But what?"

"It costs twelve rubles."

"Well?"

"We have not got them."

And indeed we had not got twelve rubles.

I thought it very sad not to have twenty-five thousand rubles, nor even twelve rubles, when I required them.

I resolved to telegraph to my mother.

Feeling sad and perplexed, I went to the telegraph office and sat down at a table to write my message:

"Mother, dear, we are unhappy and forlorn; Tioka and I want to come home and stay with you always. Please send us at once—"

I was meditating on what sum to mention, when I felt the touch of a hand upon my shoulder. Startled, I turned, and raised my eyes. Before me stood a man—dark, rather tall, with a brown mustache and pendulous cheeks. Surely I knew him! Where had I seen that face before? Suddenly there flashed into my mind the recollection of a crowded, brilliantly lighted restaurant. I saw Vassili, amid much laughter, counting the dark-eyed tziganes to see if one of them were missing—*Prilukoff!* "The Scorpion!" It was he who stood before me.

"Countess Tarnowska! Who would have dreamt of finding you here!" he exclaimed. "What are you doing in Moscow?"

"I—I do not know," I stammered. I had in fact not infrequently asked myself what I was doing in Moscow.

"I have heard of all your misfortunes," he said, lowering his voice, and gazing at me sympathetically. "I have read the papers and heard all the fuss. Come now, come," he added, "you must not weep. Let us go and have tea at the Métropole; there we can talk together." And he took me familiarly by the arm.

I drew back. "I wanted to telegraph—," I began.

"Telegraph? To whom?" inquired Prilukoff with an authoritative air.

"To my mother."

"Why? What do you want to telegraph to her for?"

I flushed. "I—I have no money—" I stammered.

"Well, I have," said Prilukoff, and he drew me out of the office.

At the top of the steps he stopped and looked me in the face. "What a fortunate meeting!" he said. "Our lucky star must have brought it about." With these words his brown eyes looked straight into mine. "Our lucky star!" he repeated.

Merciful heaven, why did not a whisper, not a breath of warning come to me then? Why did no tremor in my soul admonish me, no heavenly inspiration hold me back? Nothing, nothing checked the smile upon my lips, nor the words in which I gaily answered him:

"Our lucky star! So be it." And I took his arm.

The die of my destiny was cast. I went out on my way to destruction and ruin.

There were many people and much music in the Métropole when we entered.

It is strange to think how all the memorable and significant hours of my life are associated in my mind with the entrancing rhythm of dance-music, with the lilting tunes of waltz, mazurka and polonaise.

All the tragedies, all the extravagances that convulsed my existence bloomed up like tragic modern flowers in the hothouse of some fashionable restaurant, under the feverish breath of a tzigane orchestra.

So great became the power of this obsession over me, that no sooner did I enter a restaurant where there were people, and lights, and the music of stringed instruments, than I straightway felt as if I had lost my senses. Under the influence of such an atmosphere all my thoughts assumed disordered and extravagant forms. The tones of the violins excited and electrified me; as the bows swept the quivering strings I also quivered and vibrated, shaken with indescribable perturbation. The waves of sound seemed to envelop me in a turbid vortex of sentiment and sensibility.

Ah, if there had been more silence in my life, more shade, more seclusion! It is not within the safe walls of the home, not at one's own peaceful and inviolate hearth that perversity stirs to life and catastrophe is born.

Oh! Tania, my only daughter, if the wishes of your sorrowful mother could but reach you and her prayers for you be granted, they would encompass with shade and silence your young and virginal heart.

And I—ah, if I could but go back to the white vacant land of childhood, I would kneel down and entreat from heaven naught else but shade and silence in my life. . . .

But in the Café Métropole the blazing lights were lit, the orchestra was swinging its unhallowed censer of waltz-music through the perfumed air and the Scorpion was sitting before me drinking his tea and laughing.

"Do you remember how much afraid you were of me at the Strelna, when I jumped from the divan and touched your shoulder? And afterwards—when you found me asleep at the bottom of the sleigh?"

Yes, I remembered.

"And now you are no longer afraid of me?"

No. Now I was no longer afraid of him.

Fate, the Fury, standing behind me, must have laughed as with her nebulous hand she covered my smiling eyes.

XXI

WHAT charmed and delighted me most in the Scorpion was a pet phrase of his that he was constantly using: *"Leave that to me!"*

He said it every minute, a hundred times a day. Occasionally there might be a slight variation; he might say, "Don't trouble your head about that"; or "Never mind, I 'll see to it." But as a rule it was the brief enchanting sentence: "Leave that to me."

I cannot possibly describe the sense of utter relief and comfort with which those few words inspired me. I felt unburdened, as it were, exonerated, set free from every responsibility, from every anxiety, almost from every thought. It was as if Prilukoff had said of my very soul, "Leave it to me," so complete was my sense of tranquil relinquishment.

In truth I had never given much thought to the practical side of life. No sense of responsibility had ever weighed upon my narrow shoulders; there had always been so many people around me to give me advice, to direct me, to think and to act on my behalf!

When I had suddenly found myself alone in the world with Tioka and Elise I had felt more frightened and more helpless than they. But now, here once more was some one ready to direct me, ready to think and act and decide for me. Occasionally, realizing my position, I exclaimed anxiously: "Dear me, what shall I do about money?"

Prilukoff would answer briefly: "Leave that to me."

"But how shall I pay my bills?"

"Leave your bills to me."

"And how shall I prevent Vassili from robbing me of Tioka?"

"Don't bother about Tioka. Leave him to me."

"And, oh dear! I wish I could be divorced from Vassili."

"You shall be divorced; I shall see to it."

"But what will my mother say?"

"Leave your mother to me."

There seemed to be nothing in the world that could not be left to the omniscient and all-sufficing care of Donat Prilukoff. I was deeply moved and grateful.

"How shall I ever be able to thank you?"

"Leave the thanking to me," said Prilukoff.

For a long time, indeed, he seemed neither to desire nor expect any gratitude. He looked after my interests, my divorce, my parents, my son, my maid, my debts, and my health. But he asked for no thanks; all he required was that I should be docile and content.

It was a period of respite. Soon I forgot that I had ever thought of him as a Scorpion or an octopus. Indeed, he was to my eyes a strange and delightful mixture of knight errant, of guardian saint, of commissionaire and hero.

I did not feel then that every favor, every counsel I asked of him, was but another link in the subtle chain that bound me to him.

Soon I was unable to do anything without asking for his opinion and his assistance. Tioka, Elise and I grew accustomed to see him arrive with his masterful air and brisk greeting every afternoon; then every morning; then every evening as well. We never went out without him; no letter was received or written without its being given to him to read.

If Tioka broke a toy, if Elise was overcharged in an account, if I received an anonymous letter, it was immediately referred to Prilukoff. He put everything into his pocket, saying: "Leave that to me."

And, true to his word, he mended the toys, he adjusted the accounts, he discovered and punished my anonymous slanderers. He was astute, deliberate and intelligent.

I felt convinced that he was also kind and generous and good.

Who can say that in those days he was not so? The dreadful Prilukoff, assassin and blackmailer, who turned against me, livid with wrath, in the court-room at Venice, was he—could he be?—the same Prilukoff who, in those far-off days, mended little Tioka's playthings? Who was so anxious if he saw me looking pale? Of whom Elise, clasping her work-worn hands, used to say: "When he appears he seems to me like Lohengrin!"

Lohengrin! How bitterly I smile, remembering all that ensued. And yet—I cannot believe it. I cannot understand it. Which of those two beings —the maleficent demon or the chivalrous knight— was the real Prilukoff?

Perhaps, when these sinister years of prison and sorrow are past that cancel in their flight so many things, and shed light upon so many others, some day he may cross my path again. Shall I then not discern in his faded, grief-stricken face the strong and compassionate Lohengrin of long ago? . . .

Meanwhile I drifted on, submissive to my fate.

Only two things perturbed me. One was the

fear lest Tioka should be taken from me—an anguish that was with me day and night. The other was a torturing secret, which I confided to no one. It was—how shall I say it?—my terror of closed doors!

Every time I found myself alone in front of a closed door, I did not dare to open it. I had the fixed, frightful idea that behind the door I should see—Bozevsky! I had the irremovable conviction that he was standing, motionless and expectant, behind every door that confronted me. All the doors of our apartment had to be kept wide open. If it ever happened that I found myself alone in a room of which the door was closed, instead of opening it I rang the bell, I called, I cried for help; and if it chanced that every one was out, or no one heard me, I stood riveted to the spot, rigid with fear, staring at the terrifying mystery of that closed door before me. Perchance, with a great effort of will, holding my breath while the beads of cold perspiration started on my brow, I ventured to put out my hand towards the handle—but in an instant I found myself pushing the door to again, leaning desperately with all my strength against the frail barrier which concealed—oh, I knew it did!—Bozevsky, standing upright and terrible, with the yellow gauze round his neck.

This notion, horrible as it was in the daytime, became an unbearable fear after nightfall. Tioka went upstairs to bed, accompanied by Elise, at about eight o'clock. Twice it happened that, when they were both asleep, a draught caught the open door of the drawing-room in which I was sitting, and shut it. With chattering teeth, and shivers running over me like chilly water, I remained there, motionless, through all the hours of the night, knowing that Bozevsky was there, separated from me only by that slender wooden partition.

In the morning Elise found me lying on the floor in a faint.

One day Elise was summoned to Neuchâtel. Her father was at the point of death, and wished to give his last embrace and blessing to his only daughter. It was five o'clock in the afternoon when the telegram for Elise arrived; at eight o'clock, distracted and weeping, she was in the train.

Tioka and I, who had accompanied her to the station, returned homeward feeling sad and lonely. We felt doubly lonely that day, as Donat Prilukoff had been obliged to leave Moscow on account of a lawsuit, and was not to return until the following evening.

We had, it is true, another serving-woman, a

cook; but she left us every evening to go and sleep at her own home.

We entered our dark and silent apartment nervously. I hastily turned on all the lights and then carried Tioka, who was cross and already half asleep, up the inner staircase leading to our bedrooms.

I undressed him and put him to bed, tucking him up warmly and comfortably.

"Oh, dear," he sighed, rubbing his eyes; "do you think the wolves will come and eat me if I don't say my prayers to-night?"

"No, no, dearest. I will say them for you. Go to sleep."

I kissed him and turned out the light; then I went downstairs to get a book from the library, intending to return to my room at once. I felt nervous and restless. I was afraid I should not be able to sleep.

How did it happen? Perhaps it was an instant's forgetfulness that caused me to draw the door of the library after me. It closed with a heavy thud. The long, dark-red curtain turned on its rod and fell in front of the doorway.

I was imprisoned!

XXII

I should never dare to leave that room.

Suddenly I thought that Tioka might call me. But between him and me, standing outside on the threshold of that draped door, was there not the man whom I had seen die in Yalta? Horrifying memory! For a long time I did not venture to stir. I turned my head and looked behind me, then fixed my eyes afresh on the red curtain. Suddenly I thought I heard a cry.

Yes; it was Tioka calling me, Tioka all alone upstairs, who was frightened too, frightened even as I was. With shivers swathing me from head to foot as with an icy sheet, I listened to those cries which every moment grew shriller and wilder. Then, in answer to him, I screamed too.

Oh, those shrieks ringing through the empty house—shrieks which only that silent ghost behind the door could hear!

Suddenly another thrill ran through me; the electric bell had sounded. Some one was ringing at our door; some one was coming to save us. Tioka still screamed, and the bell continued to ring.

I could also hear blows on the door and then a voice—Prilukoff's voice—calling: "It is I. Open the door!"

With a sob of mingled terror and joy I thrust back the curtain and flung open the dreaded door. Stumbling blindly through the passage I reached the hall door and drew back the latch. Prilukoff stood on the threshold; he was pale as death.

"What has happened?" he cried. "What is the matter?" And he gripped my arm.

I was sobbing with joy and relief. "Tioka, Tioka!" I called out. "Don't cry any more. Donat has come! We are here, we are near you!"

Tioka's cries ceased at once.

But Prilukoff still held me fast. "What has happened?" he asked, clenching his teeth.

"I was afraid, I was afraid—" I gasped.

"Of whom?"

A fresh outburst of tears shook me. "Of the dead," I sobbed.

"Leave the dead to me," said Prilukoff.

He entered and shut the door.

.   .   .   .

Thus, unconscious and unwilling, I descended yet another step down the ladder of infamy.

Shrinking and reluctant I trailed my white garments into defilement, sinking with every step deeper into the mire which was soon to engulf me; the mire which was to reach my proud heart, my pearl-encircled throat, my exalted brow on which nobility had set its seal in vain.

It was about that time, I remember, that Delphinus, a renowned fortune-teller, came to Moscow. One morning, having nothing else to do, I went with the smiling, skeptical Elise to consult him in his luxurious apartments.

He took both my hands and gazed for a long time at a crystal ball which was before him. Then he said: "Woman, your life is a tragedy."

I smiled, incredulous yet disturbed. "Pray say rather a comedy, if you can."

He shook his head. "A tragedy," he repeated gloomily. Then he uttered several commonplaces which might apply to any other woman as well as to me. Finally, with knitted brows, he looked still more closely into the crystal. "Two men," he said, speaking slowly, "have yet to enter into your life. One will bring salvation, the other ruin. Choose the one, and you will attain happiness; choose the other and you will perish."

He paused. "You will choose the other," he said, and released my hand.

I got up, smiling. "Oh, no, indeed! Now that I have been forewarned—"

"You will choose the other," he repeated oracularly. "It is your destiny."

Although I am not really superstitious, this curt, obscure prediction impressed me strangely.

"I shall beware of whom I meet," I said to myself; and indeed, every time a man spoke to me, even casually, I wondered: could this be the One? —or the Other?

But days and months passed, and I made no new acquaintances.

Prilukoff kept me jealously secluded, and little Tioka absorbed my every hour. Apart from these two I saw no one at all.

It was by mere chance that one day I met a former acquaintance.

I had taken Tioka for a walk in the park when we saw a gentleman and a child sitting on a bench in the shade. They were both dressed in deep mourning, and they looked sad and disconsolate. The little boy was leaning his fair head on his father's arm, watching him as, with an air of melancholy abstraction, he traced hieroglyphics in the gravel with his stick. On hearing us approach the man in mourning raised his head and looked at us.

I recognized him at once. It was Count Paul Kamarowsky, the husband of one of my dearest friends, who lived at Dresden, and whom I had not seen for nearly two years.

He recognized me, too, and started to his feet with eager face, while the little boy looked at us diffidently, still holding to his father's sleeve.

"Countess Tarnowska!" he exclaimed, holding out both his hands.

I laid my hand in his; as he clasped it between his black-gloved fingers a slight shiver ran through me. I turned to the pale little child beside him who was still glancing up at me timidly. "Is this Grania?"

"Yes. It is Grania," said Count Kamarowsky. Then he perceived my questioning glance at his mourning. "Poor Emilia—" he began, but his voice broke.

"Poor Emilia?" Was it possible that my little school friend of long ago, the fair-haired, laughter-loving Lily should now be "poor Emilia," to be spoken of in solemn, mournful tones? I could hardly believe it. I seemed to see her still, bending over her 'cello with her fair curls tumbling over her face as she played her favorite Popper tarantelle. . . . I could see her laughing with mischievous eyes agleam behind her flaxen locks, like dark stars seen through a golden cloud. And here, clad in mourning for her, her husband and child stood before me.

Great tenderness and pity filled my heart.

Tioka had gone close to Grania, and the two children were looking at each other with that expression of simple gravity which is so far removed from the conventional smile with which grown-up people greet each other for the first time. Their gaze was serious, thoughtful and interrogative.

"Do you like pelicans?" Tioka inquired suddenly.

"No," said Grania.

"Neither do I," said Tioka; and there was a long silence.

"Do you like ducks?" asked Tioka.

"Yes," replied Grania.

"So do I," said Tioka; and their friendship was sealed.

Count Kamarowsky and I were less prompt in discovering a community of tastes such as that which so quickly linked our two children together. This grave silent man in his widower's garb was almost a stranger to me. As we parted he asked permission to call. But on the following day a telegram from my father summoned me to Otrada. My mother was ill and desired my presence.

XXIII

It was a hurried departure and an anxious journey. We arrived late in the evening at my father's house. He came to meet us at the gate, tall and solemn, his white hair stirred by the wind. He kissed me without speaking and laid his hand on Tioka's head.

"Mother—?" I scarcely dared to inquire.

"Better. She is better. She has improved greatly since she knew you were coming."

Tioka had hurriedly kissed his grandfather's hand, and now was hastening up the great staircase to see his grandmother, to whom he was passionately attached. Soon his rippling laughter and his nimble footsteps could be heard all over the house, and my mother said that the happiness of it had well-nigh cured her.

It was scarcely daybreak next morning when Tioka came to call me to go down with him into the garden.

The great garden at Otrada—the garden of my girlhood—glowed in all its summer splendor, and Tioka ran before me with cries of joy at everything he saw.

"Look at the water! Look at the little bridge! Did you play here when you were little? Were you ever really little?" He looked at me doubtfully. "I mean really quite little—like Tania."

The mention of his sister's name was like a blow to my heart. But Tioka was already flying across the lawn.

"Oh," he cried. "There's the swing! I had forgotten there was a swing! Hurrah!"

"Hush, hush, dearest," I warned; "don't disturb grandmama who is ill."

He swung backwards and forwards, careless and handsome, shaking his blond hair in the wind.

"Grandmama cannot hear me; she is fast asleep still. And besides she is not ill any more now that we are here; otherwise grandpapa would not have gone to Kieff to-day." Tioka jumped down from the swing and raised his face to me with adorable seriousness. "Tell me, mother, when one is ill with nervousness doesn't that mean that you want something you haven't got? Then if you get it you are well again, aren't you? Grandmama wanted us. We came. And now she is cured." After a pause he went on: "I think I am ill with nervousness too. I am nervous for a bowl of goldfish; and for a hunting dog like that one," he added, indicating a large setter lying stretched in the sun with his muzzle on his paws.

"Why, that is Bear!" I cried, "our old Bear." I bent down to caress him. "Dear Bear, good Bear! Don't you recognize me?"

Bear raised his languid, blood-shot eyes, but did not stir.

"How sad he looks," I said, touching his muzzle to see whether his nose was hot. "Perhaps he is ill."

"Perhaps he is nervous, too," said Tioka. "Very likely he is nervous because he wants a bone." And the child broke into a peal of shrill, merry laughter.

In an instant the great dog had turned and leaped upon him. Snarling and growling he tore at his clothes, covering his shoulders and breast with blood-stained foam.

Tioka fell shrieking to the ground. I flung myself upon the frenzied animal, seizing him by the collar, by the ears, and striving to drag him back; but with hoarse growls and snappish barks the dog kept biting and tearing the child's garments as he lay prostrate and inert on the gravel. With one hand I clutched the neck of the dog, while with the other I picked up a stone and beat him on the head with it until the blood ran.

With a roar like that of a tiger, the animal turned and sprang upon me.

I felt the sting of his fang as it bit into my arm, and I struck his nose with the stone which was already covered with blood. With a cry of pain that had almost a human sound, the dog released his hold, turned and went off.

I saw him trotting away along the path, surly and dreadful, with his tail hanging down and his wounded head showing red in the sunshine.

I picked up the moaning, sobbing Tioka and ran with him to the house.

"Don't cry! don't cry, my darling," I implored him, myself in tears. "Don't let poor grandmama hear you! It will kill her." And Tioka tried his best to cry more softly. We crossed the courtyard to the servants' entrance, and I ran into the kitchen where the servants came thronging round us in alarm.

"The dog—," I panted, "the dog has bitten us —do you think it will give us hydrophobia?" With a groan I dropped little Tioka into a chair; he was a pitiable sight in his torn and blood-stained garments.

The women and the two moujiks wrung their hands. "Oh, Lord! Oh, Lord! What shall we do? With the master at Kieff and the Countess ill in bed!"

The cook had filled a basin with boiling water and was laving Tioka's wounds, while he screamed with the redoubled pain.

I knew it was necessary to do something instantly. But what? I remembered having read in the life of the three Brontë sisters that one of those heroic girls had been bitten by a mad dog, and that she herself, without disturbing her sister, who was ill with consumption, had heated an iron red-hot and had cauterized her own wounds.

"Put an iron in the fire!" I said, pointing with trembling hand to the poker.

The dismayed women did so, and I bared my arm and little Tioka's lacerated shoulder.

But when I had the terrible instrument with its glowing point in my hand, my courage failed. Tioka was shrieking with terror like a poor little maddened creature, and the women were on their knees, weeping and praying.

Alas, I am not a heroine; I threw away the red-hot iron; we bound up the wounds—which, after they had been washed, looked insignificant and harmless enough—and determined to go to Kieff at once and consult a doctor. We went upstairs on tip-toe to my mother's room. She was still sleeping quietly, with her small, pinched face sunk in the pillow.

We did not venture to wake her and tell her our terrifying story. We left orders with the servants that they were to say my father had summoned us to meet him in Kieff; and we started.

All the way I watched Tioka with the deepest anxiety. I also probed my own feelings intently, wondering whether I felt any desire to bark. I cannot say that I did. Also, during the entire journey, I kept on showing Tioka glasses of water, but he did not seem to feel any the worse for them; nor did I. This comforted us a little.

As soon as we reached Kieff I telegraphed to Prilukoff:

"Both of us bitten by mad dog. What shall we do?"

He replied: *"All right. Leave it to me."*

And, indeed, he arrived immediately and took us to Doctor Fritkof, who gave us injections of antirabic serum for three weeks. It made us feel very ill. Every minute I asked Tioka: "Do you feel inclined to bite any one?"

He invariably replied in the affirmative, which made me very miserable.

XXIV

ALTHOUGH Tioka and I both recovered, this alarming incident had its consequences on my life. It caused me to leave my old home, and from the moment of that departure I never saw my dear mother again.

With the passing of her mild and tender presence all that still was pure and holy vanished out of my life.

I was already on the brink of perdition. Freed from the restraint of that gentle hand, whose light touch even from afar had still controlled my heart, I plunged forward to destruction.

The inheritance was divided, and my share was dissipated I know not how. I returned to Moscow, and found myself ever more and more in need of money.

I lived luxuriously, I dressed gorgeously, and traveled from one place to another—yet I had nothing of my own except an income of four thousand rubles a year, which were scarcely paid to me before they were swallowed up in the gulf of my debts. I asked Prilukoff for money, and he gave it to me.

But there came a day when, on my asking him for five thousand rubles, he turned upon me abruptly.

"I have not got them," he said. "At least," he added, "not unless I steal them."

"How dreadful," I exclaimed in terror. "How can you say such a thing?" Then I laughed, feeling sure that he had spoken in jest.

"Get them from Kamarowsky," said Prilukoff, curtly.

I started with indignation. From Kamarowsky! Never, never, as long as I lived. I had seen him frequently during the last few days; he and his charming little son, Grania, still in their deep mourning and with pale, sad faces, used to come and see me, and talk to me with many tears about their dear one who was gone. It would have been horrible, it would have been indecorous, to ask Kamarowsky for money.

"I did not say you were to ask him for it," retorted Prilukoff.

"What then?"

"Telephone and invite him to dine with you to-morrow."

"Well? And then?"

"Then we shall see."

As he insisted I complied reluctantly.

Kamarowsky accepted the invitation with touching gratitude, and a large basket of roses preceded his arrival.

Prilukoff, who was still hanging about in my boudoir, but declared that he would not stay to dinner, sniffed the roses with a cynical smile:

"Flowers! Flowers! Nothing but flowers! *Nous allons changer tout cela.*"

The door bell rang, announcing the arrival of my visitor.

"What am I to do with him now he is here?" I asked Prilukoff uneasily. "What shall I say?"

"Do nothing and say nothing. And mind you don't open any letter in his presence."

"Any letter?" I asked, in bewilderment. "What letter?"

"I tell you not to open any. That is enough." With this obscure injunction Prilukoff urged me towards the drawing-room, and I went in to receive my guest.

Count Kamarowsky, while inspiring me with the deepest pity, frequently irritated and annoyed me. His grief for his lost Emilia was doubtless deep and sincere; but sometimes when I tried to console him I seemed to read in his tear-filled eyes an emotion that was not all sorrow, and in the clasp of his hand I perceived a fervor that spoke of something more than gratitude. I felt hurt for the sake of my poor friend, Lily, so lately laid to her rest; and I shrank from him with feelings akin to anger and aversion.

Yet, when I saw him moving away, pale in his deep mourning, leading his sad little child by the hand, my heart was touched and I would call them back to me and try to comfort them both. The child clung to me with passionate affection, while his father seemed loth ever to leave my side.

Conversation between us always soared in the highest regions of ethereal and spiritual things; our talk was all on abstract subjects, dwelling especially on the immortality of the soul, the abode of the departed, the probabilities of reunion in the world beyond. The commonplace everyday prose of life was so far removed from our intercourse that I felt shy of having asked him to dinner. To eat in the presence of so much sorrow seemed indecorous and out of keeping. Nevertheless, as I had invited him to dine I could not but seat myself opposite him at the flower-decked, fruit-laden table.

A man-servant, lent to me for the occasion by

Prilukoff, handed the zakusta and the vodka; and soon in the mellow atmosphere of the little dining-room, under the gentle luster of the pink-shaded lamps, a rare smile blossomed timidly now and then out of the gloom of our melancholy conversation.

We had scarcely finished taking our coffee when, to my astonishment, Prilukoff was announced. He entered with rapid step, holding a large sealed envelope in his hand. For a moment he seemed disconcerted at finding that I was not alone, and looked as if he would hide the letter behind his back. Then, with a slight shrug of the shoulders, as if acquiescing in the unavoidable presence of a stranger, he handed me the envelope with a deep bow.

"What is it?" I asked in surprise.

Prilukoff glanced somewhat uneasily at my guest, then he bent forward and said in a low voice —yet not so low that the other could not hear what he said:

"This morning, Countess, you did me the honor of confiding to me the fact that you needed ten thousand rubles. I shall be most grateful and honored if you will accept that sum from me." So saying, he placed the envelope in my hand. Then with a brief salutation to Count Kamarowsky and another profound bow to me, he pleaded haste and withdrew.

A flush had mounted to the Count's temples.

"Who was that?" he asked in a harsh voice.

I mentioned Prilukoff's name, and Kamarowsky with knitted eyebrows exclaimed: "You must have very confidential relations with him, if he permits himself to give you ten thousand rubles."

"Oh, no—no," I stammered. "He is—he is only lending them to me. I shall pay them back, of course—"

Kamarowsky had risen from his chair. He took both my hands and pressed them to his breast.

"How wrong of you! How wrong! Why did you not ask me? Have you no confidence in me? How can you accept assistance from a stranger when I am here—I, who am so devoted to you?"

I know not why I burst into tears. A sense of shame and degradation overcame me. In a moment his arms were round me.

"Dearest, sweetest, do not cry. I know you must feel humiliated at accepting money from that man, who may afterwards make all kinds of claims upon you. Return the money to him, I implore you, and accept it from me."

I could not answer for my tears.

"Promise me that you will give it back," Kamarowsky went on, clasping me closer to him. "If you refuse me this favor I shall go away and you shall never see me again. For the sake of our Emilia—for the sake of little Grania—accept it from me. And let me be your friend from now on and forever."

It took a long time to reconcile me to the sense of my own debasement.

He wrote out a check to me for ten thousand rubles and put it into my hands. He closed my fingers forcibly over it, pressing them closely and thanking me in a moved voice.

Then he went away, and I was left alone with the check and Prilukoff's sealed envelope.

I had wanted five thousand rubles and here I was with twenty thousand before me!

Poor, good Kamarowsky! And poor, dear, kind Prilukoff!

"I do not see why I should really return this to Prilukoff!" I said to myself.

I broke the seals and opened the envelope that he had presented to me with so much solemnity. Petrified with astonishment I gazed at its contents. Then I laughed softly.

"On the whole, I think I *will* return it," I said, and laid the envelope aside.

It was full of old newspaper cuttings!

XXV

Facilis descensus Averni.

My downfall was rapid and irretrievable.

I soon became familiar with expedients and intrigues, I trod the tortuous paths that lead down into the valley of dishonor. For the outside world I might still appear a person of distinction, I might still call myself the Countess Tarnowska, but I had ceased to be that simple, ordinary, peerless being—an honest woman. I seemed to be surrounded by that peculiar atmosphere which envelops the adventuress as in an invisible mist— that imperceptible emanation by which persons of repute are instinctively repelled, and which draws within its ambit the idler and adventurer, the depredator and outcast of society.

I had accepted money to which I had no claim. From this want of dignity to the want of rectitude how brief is the step! Between indiscretion and transgression how uncertain is the boundary! And suddenly there comes a day when one awakes to find oneself—a criminal!

Ah, then we stop short in horror. We look back

and see the abyss, the impassable gulf that henceforward separates us from the distant, candid
summits of innocence. How has it been possible
for us to travel along that vertiginous road which
knows no return? What evil spirits have band-
aged our eyes, have placed for our feet bridges and
stepping stones so that almost without noticing it
we have crossed ravines and precipices which
never in this life we may traverse again? We can
but go forward and downward: we can turn back
no more.

Not at this period did I realize the irrevocable
character of the fate I had chosen. Rather did I
seem to perceive a new life opening out before me,
leading me back once more to rectitude and honor,
a return to that peaceful, conventional existence
so often scorned by those who lead it, so bitterly
regretted and desired by those who have forfeited
and forsaken it.

Prilukoff still held me bound to him by the triple
bonds of gratitude, of affection and of complicity.
But Count Kamarowsky was swaying me towards
a brighter and securer future. My marriage with
Vassili, so long merely an empty and nominal tie,
was about to be dissolved by a decree from the
Holy Synod, and Kamarowsky implored me to
marry him. His sadness and the loneliness of his

little son moved me deeply; the thought of bringing light and joy into their lives was unspeakably sweet to me, while for my part I rejoiced to think that by the side of a worthy and honorable man I might take my place in the world once more, rehabilitated and redeemed. With Prilukoff, as I could see, downfall and ruin were imminent. He had left Moscow for a few days; but he would return, and alas! he would resume his dominion over me. I knew that with him the ultimate plunge into dishonor was inevitable.

And so with bitter tears of repentance, clasping the two fair heads of Tioka and Grania to my breast, I vowed to Heaven that I would be to them both a tender and a faithful mother, worthy of the lofty duty that by Divine grace was to be once more assigned to me.

Count Kamarowsky's gratitude and joy were boundless.

"You are giving back life to me," he said, his kind eyes shining with emotion. "I do not feel worthy of so much happiness."

"Don't, don't!" I said, turning away my face and flushing deeply at the thought of my recent unprincipled life. "It is I, I who am unworthy—"

But Kamarowsky interrupted me.

"Hush, Marie, hush. I know that you have suf-

fered much and that you have been led astray.
But let the dead past bury the past. All I ask of
you is the pure white page of the future.''

"You are generous, you are kind,'' I said, and
tears burned in my eyes. ''But let me tell you,
let me tell you all—''

''Mura,'' he said, calling me by the tender pet-
name of my childhood, ''do not raise impassable
barriers between us. What I have no knowledge
of does not exist so far as I am concerned. The
unknown is but a shadow; and I am not afraid
of shadows. But if to that shadow you give a
living shape and a name, it will rise between you
and me, and I shall not be able to clasp you in my
arms until I have destroyed it. Speak if you
must. But, for our happiness, it were far better
for you to keep silence—and to forget.''

''Ah, you are right! Let there be no more
sorrow, no more tragedies around me. Take me
away from Moscow, away from all who know me.
I will keep silence, and forget.''

Our departure from Moscow was like a flight.
I left a letter for Prilukoff, entreating him to forgive and forget me, begging him not to debar me
from taking my way again towards safety and
rehabilitation. I expressed to him my sympathy,
my gratitude and regret; and I implored him in

the name of all that he still held dear or sacred to return to his family and to his career, to the lofty and straightforward course of honor from which I, unhappy creature that I was, had unwittingly, unwillingly turned him aside.

Kamarowsky took us to the Riviera—from the snows of the north to the fragrant orange-groves of Nice and Hyères. The tinkling of sleighs gliding through the blue-cold streets of Moscow still seemed to ring in my ears when, lo! the lazy, sun-warm silence of the south enwrapped my senses in its languorous sweetness. The two children, dazed with the heat and the blueness around them, stood in amazement, with hands clasped and mouths open, at the sight of the golden oranges and the huge foliage of cacti and aloes, thinking that by some wonder-working charm they had been carried into fairyland.

The distant sails, aslant on the radiant indigo of the sea, looked like white butterflies poised on a stupendous flower of lapis lazuli. . . .

For three brief days I thought that fate had not overtaken me, and that my sins would not find me out.

My sins! As in the old German fable the children are led into the depths of a forest, and left there to be lost and forgotten—even so did I think

that my sins would be lost and forgotten, even so
did I think that they would never issue again from
the shade in which I had hidden them.

Smiling, I moved forward to meet the future,
exalted by the affection of an honorable man,
purified by the love of two innocent children.

And I said in my heart: "Fate is pitiful and
God has shown mercy. He has suspended His
judgment and has allowed me one last chance. I
shall not be found wanting; I shall be worthy of
His clemency."

Then lo! at a turning in my pathway, the forgotten avengers stand before me; my sins, like
spectral furies, have found me out!

We were finishing dinner on the terrace of the
Bellevue at Hyères, my betrothed and I. The
children had said good night, had kissed and embraced us and run off, chattering and twittering
with Elise, to their rooms. Kamarowsky had just
lit a cigarette, and was leaning over to me with a
word of tenderness, when I perceived immediately
behind him at a neighboring table—a face, a grin-
ning, fiendish face.

My heart bounded. It was the Scorpion!

Why was it that name that first rushed to my
mind? Why was my primitive sense of fear and
repulsion renewed at the sight of him?

Ah, that man staring and grimacing at me over Kamarowsky's shoulder was not the friend, the lover, the knight of the heroic Saga whom I had known and trusted in my days of desolation; no, he was the terrifying and truculent monster of the octopus story; he was the Scorpion who years ago had filled my soul with dread.

When had he come? How long had he been sitting at that table, watching my garrulous gladness, my timorous, reawakened happiness?

XXVI

I GLANCED at him apprehensively; I tried to greet him, but he made no return to my timid salute. He was smiling with a crooked mouth, his arms crossed before him on the table. He was mocking at Kamarowsky and at me, and my terror seemed greatly to amuse him.

I rose nervously, wishing to retire, but Kamarowsky detained me.

"What is troubling you, dearest?" he asked, noticing my frightened eyes. And he turned to see what was behind him.

I trembled in prevision of a stormy scene. But the Count did not recognize Prilukoff; he had only seen him once for a few moments that evening in my drawing-room when he had brought me the mysterious sealed envelope. Now Donat had his hat on his head; and besides, with that sinister smirk distorting his face I scarcely recognized him myself.

As soon as we rose from the table, Prilukoff did the same, and passing in front of us entered the hotel before we did. I trembled, while Kamarowsky with his arm in mine led me, talking placidly and affectionately, towards the entrance of the hotel. Doubtless he intended to accompany me to my sitting-room. But what if we found Prilukoff there?

It was Elise Perrier who saved me. As we stepped out of the lift I saw her coming quickly down the corridor to meet us.

"If you please, madame," she stammered, "there is a lady—a visitor"—her lips were white as she uttered the falsehood—"who wishes to see madame. She is waiting here, in the sitting-room, and she would like to—to see your ladyship alone."

"Who is it?" asked the Count.

"I think it is the—that relation of madame's"— Elise was going red and white by turns—"that relation from—from Otrada."

"Ah, I know," I stammered breathlessly. "Aunt Sonia, perhaps." Then turning to Kamarowsky: "Will you wait for me downstairs in the reading-room?"

"Very well. Don't be long." And Count Kamarowsky turned on his heel and left us.

I went rapidly on in front of Elise, who, humiliated by the falsehood she had told, hung her head in shame both for herself and for me; and I entered my sitting-room.

On the couch, smoking a cigarette, sat Prilukoff. He did not rise when I entered. He sat there smoking and looking at me with that curious crooked smile. A great fear clutched my heart.

"Donat," I stammered, "why did you not let me know you had arrived?"

He made no answer; but he laughed loudly and coarsely, and my fear of him increased.

"Did you receive my letter? Are you cross with me?"

"Cross?" he shouted, leaping to his feet, his eyes glaring like those of a madman. "Cross? No, I am not cross." I recoiled from him in terror, but he followed me, pushing his distorted face close to mine. "You ruin a man, you drive him to perdition, and then you inquire whether he is cross. You take an honorable man in your little talons, you turn and twist him round your fingers, you mold him and transform him and turn him into a coward, a rogue, and a thief; then you throw him aside like a dirty rag—and you ask him if he is cross! Ha, ha!" And he laughed in my face; he was ghastly to look at, livid in hue, with a swollen vein drawn like a cord across his forehead.

I burst into tears. "Why—why do you say that?" I sobbed.

"Why do I say that?" stormed Prilukoff.

"Why? Because I had a wife and I betrayed her for you; I had two children and I forsook them for you; I had a career and I lost it for you; I was a man of honor and I have turned thief for you."

"Oh, no, no!" I stammered, terrified.

"What? No? No?" he exclaimed, and with trembling hands he searched his breast-pocket and drew from it a bulky roll of banknotes. "No? This I stole—and this—and this—and this—because you, vampire that you are, needed money."

"But I never told you to steal—"

"No, indeed; you never told me to steal. And where was I to get the money from? Where? Where?" So saying, he flung the banknotes in my face and they fell all over and around me. "You did not tell me to steal, no. But you wanted money, money, money. And now you have got it. Take it, take it, take it!"

I sobbed despairingly. "Oh, no, no, Donat! Have pity!"

"I have had pity," he shouted. "I have always had pity—nothing but pity. You were ill and miserable and alone, and I left my home in order to stay with you. You wept, and I comforted you. You had no money, and I stole it for you. How could I have more pity?" He was himself in tears. "And now, because I am degraded and a criminal on your account, you leave me, you fling me aside and you marry an honest man. And I may go to perdition or to penal servitude."

"Do not speak like that, I implore you."

"Ah, but Countess Tarnowska, if I go to penal servitude, so shall you. I swear it. I am a thief and may become a murderer; but if I go to prison, you go too." He collapsed upon the sofa and hid his face in his hands.

As I stood looking down upon him I saw as in a vision the somber road to ruin that this man had traversed for my sake, and I fell on my knees at his feet.

"Donat! Donat! Do not despair. Forgive me, forgive me! Go back, and return the money you have taken; go back and become an honest man again!"

He raised a haggard face in which his wild, bloodshot eyes seemed almost phosphorescent.

"There is no going back. By this time all Moscow knows that I have absconded, and carried off with me the money that was confided to my care."

"But if you go back at once and return it?"

"I am ruined all the same. I am utterly lost and undone. Who would ever place their trust in me again? Who would every rely upon my honor? No, I am a criminal, and every one knows it. The brand of infamy is not to be cancelled by a flash of tardy remorse. I am done for. I am a thief, and that is all there is about it."

A thief! I had never seen a thief. In my imagination thieves were all slouching, unkempt roughs, with caps on their heads, and colored handkerchiefs tied round their throats. And here was this gentleman in evening dress—this gentleman who had been introduced to me as a celebrated and impeccable lawyer, who had been my lover, and Tioka's friend, and Elise's Lohengrin—and he was a thief!

I could not believe it.

At that moment a voice was heard outside. It was one of the bell-boys of the hotel; he was passing through the corridor calling: "Forty-seven! Number forty-seven."

Prilukoff started. "Forty-seven? That is the number of my room. Who can be asking for me? Who can know that I am here?"

In his eyes there was already the look of the fugitive, the startled flash of fear and defiance of the hunted quarry.

I looked round me at all the banknotes scattered on the carpet, and I felt myself turn cold. "Hide them, hide them," I whispered, wringing my hands.

"Hide them yourself!" he answered scornfully.

I heard footsteps in the corridor. They drew near. They stopped. Some one knocked at the door. Terror choked my throat and made my knees totter.

I stooped in haste to pick up all the money while Prilukoff still looked at me without moving. I held it out to him in a great heap of crumpled paper. But still he did not stir.

Again the knocking was repeated. Who could it be? Kamarowsky? The police? I opened a desk and flung the bundle of banknotes into it.

Then I said, "Come in."

XXVII

It was only a saucy little page-boy in red
uniform.

"If you please, Count Kamarowsky sends word
that he is waiting for you."

"Say that I shall be down directly."

"No," contradicted Prilukoff; "send word that
you are not going down."

"But then he will come here."

"You will say that you cannot receive him."

And that was what took place. And not on that
evening only. Prilukoff installed himself, during
long days and evenings, in my apartments, and
refused to go away. Very often he did not even
allow me to go out of the room.

Then came Count Kamarowsky knocking at the
door.

"No! no! You cannot come in!" cried Elise
Perrier, pale and trembling, leaning against the
locked door.

"But why? Why? What has happened?"

"Nothing has happened. Madame is not feeling well," Elise would reply, in quavering tones.

"But that is all the more reason why I should

see her," protested the Count. "I must see her!"

"It is impossible!" And Elise, whom fear rendered well-nigh voiceless, would roll towards me her round, despairing eyes.

Then the Count would speak to me through the closed door, entreating and arguing; and every time he used a tender expression Prilukoff, who held me fast, pinched my arm.

"Mura, Mura, let me in. Let me see you for a moment. You know how I love you (pinch); it is cruel to lock me out as if I were a stranger. If you are ill let me take care of you, with all my tenderness (pinch), with all my love (pinch)—"

In feeble accents I would reply: "Forgive me —I shall soon be better—do not trouble about me."

"But what is the matter? Why do you not want to see me? Do you not love me any more?"

"Oh, yes, I love—(pinch). Please, please go away. I shall come down as soon as I can."

Then I could hear his slowly retreating footsteps, while Prilukoff glared at me and, on general principles, pinched my arm again.

It was with the greatest difficulty that I could conceal Prilukoff's presence from little Tioka.

One day the child caught sight of him seated on the terrace, and, with a wild cry of delight, started to run towards him. I caught him in my arms.

"No, darling, no! That is not Prilukoff. It is some one very much like him; but it is not our friend."

And as the man, with scowling countenance, was gazing out at the sea, and paid no heed to us, Tioka believed me, and, with a little sigh of regret, ran in search of his playmate Grania.

The life Prilukoff led me in this grotesque and unbearable situation is impossible to describe. My days were passed in an agony of terror. When I dined with Kamarowsky, Prilukoff invariably took a seat at the next table, and I might almost say that it was he who regulated our conversation. If any subject were raised that was distasteful to him—my approaching marriage to Kamarowsky, for instance, or some tender reminiscence which my betrothed loved to recall—Prilukoff, at the adjoining table, made savage gestures which terrified me and attracted the attention of all the other guests. He would shake his fists at me, glare at me with terrible eyes, and, if I pretended not to notice him, he upset the cruet-stand or dropped his knife and fork noisily to attract my attention. He would stare at the unconscious, slightly bald head of Kamarowsky, and imitate his gestures with a demoniacal grin.

The guests of the hotel thought him insane, and

he certainly behaved as if he were. I myself have often thought: "Surely he is a madman!" when I came upon him suddenly, hidden behind the curtains in my sitting-room, or crouching in a dark corner, or lying on my bed smoking cigarettes. I felt that my nerves and my reason were giving way.

"What do you want of me, you cruel man?" I sobbed. "What am I to do? Do you wish me to tell everything to Kamarowsky? To break off the marriage and return to Moscow with you?"

"We cannot return to Moscow, and you know it," growled Prilukoff.

"Somewhere else, then. Anywhere! I will go wherever you like, I will do whatever you like. Anything, anything, rather than endure this torture any longer."

"For the present we stay here," declared Prilukoff, who seemed to enjoy my anguish. "And as for the future," he added, rolling his terrible eyes, "you can leave that to me."

Sometimes he forbade me to go out with Kamarowsky. At other times he followed us in the streets, torturing me behind the unconscious back of my betrothed, who marveled and grieved at my extraordinary and frequently absurd behavior.

Early one morning, as I looked out of my window, I saw Kamarowsky standing on the terrace, gazing thoughtfully out at the sea. I ran down to him. We were alone. "Paul," I whispered hurriedly, "let us go away from here; let us leave quietly, to-day, without saying a word to any one."

He laughed. "What a romantic idea! Do you not like this place? Are you not happy here?"

"No, Paul, no! There is some one spying upon me."

"Spying upon you?" he repeated, greatly astonished. "Is that the reason of your strange behavior?"

"Yes, yes, but do not ask me any more questions."

"Who is it? I must know who it is."

"No, Paul. I will tell you later on. Hush!"

"You are a fanciful creature," he said, laughing and patting my cheek.

I felt hurt at his calm acceptance of what I had told him, and wondered that he did not insist upon knowing more. I reflected in my folly that if he really loved me he ought to have been less satisfied and secure. I did not understand—alas! I never understood—his guileless and noble trust in me. The insensate and exacting passion of others who until now had dominated my life had spoiled me for all normal affection. Hypersensitive and

COUNT PAUL KAMAROWSKY

overwrought, I myself suffered unless I caused suffering to those I loved; nor did I ever feel sure of their love unless they doubted mine.

> The love that varies not from day to day,
> A tranquil love, unruffled and serene—

was not the love I knew. My storm-tossed heart did not recognize it. Neither on that day nor ever could I bring myself to believe that Paul Kamarowsky really loved me.

During those few moments that we were alone together on the terrace, we arranged that I should start with Tioka and Elise that very evening, during the dinner hour, leaving all our trunks behind us for my betrothed to see to after we had left. He could join us three days later in Vienna, and then we should all proceed to Orel, where important affairs claimed his presence.

Half-way through dinner, as had been arranged (and as usual Prilukoff sat at a table next to ours), Elise entered the dining-room timidly and came to our table.

"I beg your ladyship's pardon, Master Tioka is outside and wishes to say good-night."

"Bring Master Tioka in," I said, trying to speak naturally and raising my voice a little so that Prilukoff should hear.

"I am sorry, my lady, but he refuses to come," and Elise hung her head as she spoke these words; the treason we were perpetrating on Lohengrin grieved her even more, than the tortures that Lohengrin had inflicted upon me.

"Pray excuse me a moment," I said to Count Kamarowsky, and rose from the table. "I shall be back at once."

No sooner was I outside the dining-room than Elise threw my traveling cloak round me. A motor-car was throbbing at the door, and in it with beaming face sat Tioka surrounded by our hand-bags and dressing-cases, shawls and hats.

"What are we doing?" he cried gleefully. "Are we running away?"

"Yes, darling," and I clasped him to my heart, as I sank into the seat beside him. The motor was already gliding through the twilight roads towards Cannes.

"But why? Why are we running away? Have we stolen something?"

At those words my heart stopped beating. I suddenly remembered Prilukoff's ill-gotten banknotes.

"Elise!" I gasped; "in the desk in my sitting-room—there was some money."

"Yes, madame."

"What did you do with it?"

"It is quite safe, madame. I have taken it."

"You have taken it!"

"Yes, madame. Here it is." And with satisfied hand Elise patted a black leather satchel that lay in her lap.

With a sob I hid my face in my hands.

Indeed, we had stolen something!

XXVIII

As soon as we reached the frontier I telegraphed
to Prilukoff. I wanted to send Elise back to
Hyères with the money, but she refused to leave
me.

"What if Mr. Prilukoff were to kill me," she
cried. "Then what would your ladyship and poor
little Master Tioka do, all alone in the world?"

"But my good Elise, why on earth should Mr.
Prilukoff kill you?"

"I don't know," sighed Elise. "But he has
become so strange of late—" and after a pause,
she added, under her breath: "We have all become very strange."

It was true. I could not but admit it. We were
"very strange." We were not at all like other
people. The people that we met on our journeys
and in hotels, for instance, all took an interest in
external things—in the surrounding landscape, or
in works of art and monuments and cathedrals.
As for us, we never spoke about monuments. We
never entered a cathedral. We took no interest

whatever in anything beyond our own dolorous
souls. We were even as those who travel with
an invalid, watching him only, caring for and
thinking of nothing else. The invalid I traveled
with was my own sick soul.

The least peculiar among us was Count Kamarowsky. Yet even he, I fancy, was not quite like
other people. His was not a strong nature, like
that of some men I had known. Perhaps the
Slav blood is responsible for much that is abnor-
mal and unconventional. Surely we are from the
inmost depths of our nature strangely removed
from the Teutonic, the Anglo-Saxon and even the
Latin races, and our thoughts and actions must
frequently appear to them singular and incom-
prehensible.

As for Paul Kamarowsky, his dread of suffering
was so great that he preferred to know nothing
that might cause him distress. In fear lest he
should see aught that might displease him, he
chose to shut his eyes to facts and truths, pre-
ferring voluntarily to tread the easy paths of a
fool's paradise. I longed to open my heart to
him, to unburden my travailed soul and clear my
sullied conscience by a full confession; I was
ready to abide by the result, even if it meant the
loss of my last chance of rehabilitation, even

should I forfeit thereby all hope of marriage with a man of honor, rank and repute. But he closed my lips; he sealed my heart; he firmly avoided all confidences and disclosures.

"Mura," he said, "my life and yours have been too full of errors and of sorrow. Do not embitter this, our hour of joy. The past is buried; let it rest. Do not drag what is dead to the light of day again."

I bowed my head in silence. But in the depths of my conscience I knew that my past had been buried alive.

Not in my spirit alone did I suffer agonies at this period; my frail body was racked with disease and my sufferings were continuous and intense. Day by day I felt my strength decline, I saw myself wax thinner and paler; rarely indeed did an hour pass that I could count free from pain. The deep-seated ill that since the birth of my little daughter Tania had struck its fiery roots into my inmost being now bore its toxic fruits, slowly diffusing its poison through my veins. Sometimes the pangs I suffered were so acute that I cried out in anguish, while beads of cold perspiration started to my brow. But as a rule I was tortured by a deep, dull, perpetual ache, a sense of utter weakness and weariness that stifled all hope in me and all desire to live.

Oh, daughters of Eve, my purer and stronger sisters, women who have not transgressed—you whose hatred and scorn have overwhelmed me, you whose white hands have been so quick to throw the wounding stone—you alone can comprehend the agony that racked my frame, the flaming sword that pierced me, the sacred ill of womanhood that girt my body as with a sash of fire. You who in such dark hours can shelter your sufferings in the protecting shadow of your home, you who can seek refuge in a husband's tenderness and hide your stricken brow upon a faithful breast, can you not summon one throb of sorrow to your womanly hearts, one gleam of pity to your gentle eyes, when you think of the tortures I dragged from hotel to hotel, seeking to conceal my martyrdom from the inquisitive or indifferent gaze of strangers, not daring to confide in the man who loved me but who yet was almost a stranger? . . .

Who can describe the minor and yet genuine torment of the tight garments cramping the aching body; the weight of the ornate head-dress on the throbbing brow; the irony of rouge and cosmetics on the ashen cheeks; and the nauseating distaste for the rich viands that one pretends to enjoy while the noise of voices and music pierces your brain, and the glaring electric lights stab your aching eyes like a hundred knife-thrusts?

How often, on returning from some brilliant banquet to the silence and solitude of a desolate hotel bedroom, have I wept aloud with vain longing for one great joy denied to me, one supreme privilege of a happy woman: that of being weary, ill, and miserable—and yet loved all the same! How keenly have I envied some women I have known—women who were not beautiful, not brilliant and not young, but by whose sick-bed in their hour of pain a husband watched in tenderness and pity, faithful throughout the years, throughout the changes that time brings, faithful to the sad and pallid woman who had the right to lay her faded cheek upon his breast.

None, none of those who vowed they loved me, would have loved me thus! Not Vassili, not Bozevsky, not Stahl, not Kamarowsky. Prilukoff perhaps? Who knows?

But Prilukoff was a thief, a fugitive, a criminal; and day and night I prayed that he might not cross my path again.

He had not replied to my agitated telegram

informing him that Elise had unwittingly taken the money away. Nor did he, as I thought he would, join us in Vienna where we stayed several days, expecting yet dreading his arrival.

We were at a loss to know what to do with his stolen money. We did not dare to send it to him at Hyères, where I knew he had been staying under an assumed name and in constant terror of discovery. We did not dare to leave it in our rooms at the hotel. Elise carried it about with her day and night in the hated black leather satchel, which had become to us a nightmare, an incubus, an obsession. With a bitter smile I recalled the story of the English hunters in India who succeeded in capturing that most precious and sacred among all animals: a white elephant. And having captured it they knew not what to do with it. They trailed it after them across land and sea— ponderous, slow, magnificent; and nobody wanted it, and nobody knew what to do with it nor how to get rid of it. Prilukoff's stolen money was indeed a white elephant for us.

Kamarowsky with his little son had joined us in Vienna, bringing all our luggage with him. He was as boisterous as a schoolboy out for a holiday.

"There are no spies here, are there, Mura?"

he laughed, kissing my cheek loudly. "No spies to drive us away!"

Again I was hurt that he should thus make light of the mysteries of my existence. Should he not have demanded an explanation of my flight from Hyères? Should he not have insisted upon knowing who had followed me there? What love was this that could voluntarily blindfold itself and evade all explanations?

Not this, not this was the love I had dreamed of and hoped for, the steadfast refuge for my wavering spirit, the longed-for haven for my storm-tossed soul.

We proceeded almost immediately to Orel. At this period I possessed no money at all of my own; what little I had had when I left Moscow had been spent; but not for a moment did I entertain the thought of touching Prilukoff's ill-gotten wealth. Paul Kamarowsky insisted upon providing all our traveling and hotel expenses; but it was embarrassing to be unable to tip a servant or to pay for even the smallest trifle that Tioka or I might want.

I made up my mind to lay frankly before my betrothed my deplorable financial situation. And I did so on the journey to Orel. He seemed much amused at my confession; and the fact of our utter dependence upon him seemed to afford him the greatest pleasure.

He filled my purse with gold, and made me promise that I would always ask him for anything I might need or desire.

How well I remember our arrival at Orel! It was a radiant afternoon in October. Count Kamarowsky accompanied us to our hotel, where flower-filled apartments awaited us; then he left us at once to go in search of a young friend of his, the son of the Governor of Orel, who had promised to see to our passports as soon as we arrived.

I was alone in our drawing-room when Elise knocked at the door.

"The children would like to go out; they say they feel cramped from the journey," she said. "If madame allows, I will take them into the park; it is just opposite the hotel," she added.

"Certainly, Elise."

A moment later Tioka and Grania, ready to go out, came running to embrace me, and behind them Elise reappeared.

"If madame permits," she said in a low voice, "I might perhaps leave '*it*' here?"

"It" was the black leather satchel—our white elephant.

"Yes, yes; leave it," I said.

And she carried it into my bedroom and placed it on the dressing-table.

XXIX

I STEPPED out upon the balcony and watched the children cross the sunlit square; they turned and waved their hands to me; then I saw them enter the park and scamper down the shady avenue, the faithful Elise trotting quickly in their wake.

I remained on the balcony wrapped in peaceful thoughts, glad to feel the warmth of the autumn sun on my shoulders and the coolness of the autumn breeze on my cheeks. A wave of thankfulness came over me; repentance for all my past doubts and transgressions flooded my heart.

How could I ever have doubted Paul Kamarowsky's love? Was not the absolute faith he reposed in me—the blind unquestioning faith that in my folly I had often resented—was it not after all the highest homage that a noble heart could bestow? Henceforth the aim of my life should be to render myself worthy of his trust and love. In utter gratitude and devotion my heart went out to him who was about to place in my keeping the honor of

193

his unsullied name, and the care of his motherless child. I clasped my hands and breathed a fervent prayer to Heaven, a prayer that I might deserve the happiness that was in store for me.

A slight sound startled me from my reverie. It was Kamarowsky who, having returned and not finding me in the drawing-room, had knocked at my bedroom door. Receiving no reply he entered. I left the balcony, and closing the window after me, stepped into the room.

Kamarowsky was standing in front of the dressing-table holding the black leather satchel in his hand.

"What is this?" he asked casually. "Is it yours?"

The pitiless light from the window struck me full in the face, and I felt that I was turning pale. "No—no—" I stammered. "It is not mine."

"I thought not," he said, turning it round and round. "I did not remember seeing it. We had better send it down to the bureau of the hotel." And he stepped forward to touch the bell.

"No, no!" I cried, "it belongs to Elise."

"Why does Elise leave her things in your room?" Then noticing my pallor and agitation he exclaimed: "Why, dearest? What is wrong with you? You look quite white."

"It is nothing, nothing," I said, attempting to smile; and I sat down with my back to the light. I was trembling from head to foot.

He bent over me with tender solicitude. "Are you feeling ill?"

"Slightly—it will pass—it is nothing. The fatigue of the journey perhaps," and I caressed the kind face that bent over me full of affectionate concern.

He turned and rang the bell.

A waiter appeared. "Bring some brandy," ordered Kamarowsky. "Make haste. The lady is not well."

The waiter returned promptly and placed the tray on the table; as he was about to leave the room Count Kamarowsky, who was pouring out the brandy, said to him: "Wait a moment, you can take that satchel upstairs to the maid's apartment."

I sprang to my feet. "No—leave it," I cried, taking it from the waiter's hand. The man bowed and left the room.

Kamarowsky seemed astonished at my behavior. "What is the matter?" he asked. "Why are you so agitated?"

"I am not—I am not agitated at all," I stammered, trying to control my features, and holding the odious white elephant in my trembling hands.

"What on earth is in that bag?" asked the Count.

"Nothing—nothing," I said, with a vacuous, senseless smile.

"Come, now! It is full of papers," laughed Kamarowsky, putting out his hand and pressing the satchel between his fingers. "Confess, what are they? Love-letters?"

I contrived to answer his jest with a smile: "You have guessed right," I said.

"They are Elise's, I hope—not yours!" he added, half smiling and half distrustful.

I laughed. "Elise's, of course"; and with a deep sigh of relief I sank upon a chair, feeling that the danger was past. But my heart had not yet resumed its normal pulsation when the door opened and the unwitting Elise appeared on the threshold.

"We have returned, my lady, and the children have gone upstairs."

Kamarowsky jestingly took the satchel from my hand and dangled it in the air.

"Ah, Elise! What have we got in here?"

Elise rolled her eyes wildly, and a scarlet blush mounted to her face; Elise's blushes were always painful to see; now her face was of a deep damask hue.

The Count laughed. "So this is where you keep your love-letters, is it?"

"Oh, no, sir," exclaimed Elise, blushing till her eyes were filled with tears.

"What? Is this satchel not yours?"

"Oh, no, sir!—I mean—yes, sir," stuttered Elise.

Kamarowsky looked at her, and then at me. Seeing the expression of our faces the laughter faded from his lips.

"Come, Elise; tell me whose it is, and what it contains."

I attempted to make a sign to her, but the tall, broad figure of Count Kamarowsky stood between us.

I rose with a sigh of despair, acquiescing in my fate. Now—let happen what may.

"What letters are they?" insisted Kamarowsky.

I heard the hapless Elise floundering in the quicksands of falsehood; finally she let herself drift—a helpless wreck on the rock of truth.

"It is not letters, it is money," she said at last.

"Money? Money of yours?"

"No."

There was a brief silence. Then Kamarowsky said: "I do not believe you. I wish to see what it contains."

No one answered him.

"Where is the key?"

Again there was silence.

I heard a slight jingling sound; Kamarowsky was searching in his pockets for a penknife. Then he said to Elise: "You can go."

Elise went slowly and reluctantly from the room. Then I heard a faint tearing and crackling: Kamarowsky had cut through the leather of the satchel. Now the rustling of banknotes told me that he was smoothing them out on the table, and counting them.

A few moments passed.

"Thirty-five thousand rubles," said Paul Kamarowsky slowly. "I cannot understand why you should have told me you were penniless." There was an icy coldness in his voice such as I had never heard before.

"The money is not mine," I said, in trembling tones.

"Whose is it?"

How was I to answer him? Could I betray

Prilukoff? And, with him, myself? I decided to tell what was, intrinsically, the truth.

"I do not know whom it belongs to."

Once more there was silence. I wondered what he would do? Would he insult me? Would he raise his voice in bitter accusation and reproof?

No. The silence remained unbroken. Kamarowsky left the room without a word.

Ah! I was still in the grip of the octopus; its tentacles bound and crushed me still. Even from afar Prilukoff guided my destinies, drove my frail barque into storm and disaster.

With trembling hands I gathered up the scattered banknotes and thrust them back into the execrated leather bag. Ah, if only I could have freed myself from this nightmare burden, if only I could have returned the money to Prilukoff! But how? Where to? At the Bellevue, in Hyères, he had called himself Zeiler. But now where was he? Under what name was he hiding? How could I, without warning, send him such a sum of money? Where could I write to him?

No; fate had doomed me to wander through the world carrying with me the hated money in Elise's abominable satchel! At the bitterness of this thought I dropped my face in my hands and wept.

I did not hear any one knock at the door; nor

did I hear the door open.   When, still shaken with sobs, I raised my tear-stained face, I beheld standing on the threshold a stranger—a slender, fairhaired youth.   He was gazing at me with compassionate eyes, full of confusion at having found me in tears.

"Pardon me," he said, and his voice was soft and musical.

"Whom do you want?"

"I was looking for Count Kamarowsky," he replied.   "He has invited me to dine with him."   There was a pause.   "My name is Nicolas Naumoff."

"My name is Marie Tarnowska."   And I gave him my hand.

XXX

Count Kamarowsky came in shortly afterwards. He was gloomy and morose; but on seeing his friend, whom he had that morning invited to dine with us, he made a heroic effort to keep up an appearance of good temper and hospitality.

But his grief and anger were only too apparent. He sat beside me at table without speaking to me, nor did he ever turn his eyes in my direction.

Our guest seemed distressed and amazed at his behavior, and—doubtless remembering my recent tears—he gazed at me with his light-brown eyes eloquent of sympathy and compassion.

Once or twice I addressed a remark to Kamarowsky, but he scarcely answered me and I felt myself flushing and paling with humiliation.

Silence fell upon us at last. Painful and embarrassing as I felt it to be, I yet could find no word to say. A violent headache racked my temples, and I had to bite my lips to keep myself from bursting into tears.

Suddenly I got up and went into my room.
With trembling hand I sought in my dressing-case
for a bottle of cocaine, which for nearly a year I
had not touched. I lifted it to my lips and sipped
the exhilarating poison. Then I returned to the
table.

Kamarowsky was sitting grim and silent with
bent head and lowering brow, but the young
stranger raised his golden eyes under their long
fair lashes, and fixed them upon me as if to give
me comfort. After a few moments, in order to
break the well-nigh unbearable silence, he spoke
to me in his low and gentle voice.

"I hear that Delphinus, the famous crystal
gazer, has arrived in Orel. You ought to get him
to tell you your fortune."

"Is that so?" I said, smiling; and even as I
spoke the prediction of that strange soothsayer
flashed into my memory. I seemed to hear again
the brief, prophetic words: *Two men are yet to
enter into your life. One will be your salvation
—the other your ruin.*"

Two men! I glanced around me, startled and
amazed. Two men were here; one on each side
of me. Was the prophecy coming true? Were
these the two men he had spoken of? Were the
One and the Other sitting beside me now?

In my mind I could still hear the fortune-teller's nasal, dreamy accent:

"You will chose—the Other. It is your destiny."

Overcome by a feeling of timorous superstition, I looked at my two table companions, of whom One, perhaps, might represent my destruction, the Other my last hope of happiness.

At my right hand sat Kamarowsky, sullen and sinister in his grief and anger against me; on my left the young unknown, with radiant face and gold-bright eyes that smiled at me. A flash of intuition seemed to illuminate my spirit; here was salvation! Nicolas Naumoff! This unknown youth, in whose eyes I had read such complete and instant devotion—it was he whom fate had sent to lead me back to joy.

Looking back to that hour I realize that it was the rhapsodical delirium of cocaine that whipped my brain into senseless aberration; but at the time I implicitly believed that by a miracle of divination I had rent the veil of the future, and could discern with inspired gaze the distant sweep of the years to come.

I saw Kamarowsky—somber, dark, with bent head—as the very incarnation of sorrow and misfortune; and, to make assurance twice sure, was it not he whom I had chosen? And had not the diviner foretold me that he whom I chose would be the one to lead me to destruction?

But I might still draw back, I might still trick the Fates and escape from my predestined doom. With the blind impulse of the hunted quarry seeking a refuge, I turned an imploring gaze on the young unknown; he read despair in my eyes, and his own responded with a flash of comprehension; he leaned toward me, and, as if in the throe of some instant emotion, I saw him thrill from head to foot like a tense string. At this immediate response of his nerves to mine, I also felt a tremor stir me, as the water of a lake is stirred by a gust of wind. What evil spirit possessed me? Was I ill? Was I demented? I cannot tell. I know that my soul pledged itself to him at that moment; and I know that he understood me.

Thus, in my attempt to escape it, the tragic prophecy was to be fulfilled.

When Nicolas Naumoff got up to take his leave I knew that he would return, that I should see him again, and this thought intoxicated me with such delight that even Kamarowsky, in spite of his anger and his suspicions, was swept away by the radiance and rapture of my joyfulness. I was then—well may I say it now!—at the zenith of my youthful beauty, notwithstanding, or perhaps by reason of the disease that burned within me like a consuming lamp; a constant fever lit my transparent flesh into delicate rose flushes, and blazed like lighted sapphires in my translucent eyes.

I was no sooner alone with him than, seeing me thus aflame with radiant happiness, Kamarowsky rose and came towards me with outstretched hands.

"Marie, I love you, I love you! I will trust you utterly. I want to know nothing that you do not wish to tell me." And he bowed his head over my hands and kissed them.

But my wild thoughts went out to the unknown youth with the golden eyes who had left us, he through whom salvation was to come to me; and every fiber yearned for his presence. A sudden wave of almost physical repulsion for Paul Kamarowsky overcame me and I started away from his touch. "Leave me," I cried, "leave me. Let me go away." And I tried to go past him to my room.

But he stopped me, amazed and unbelieving. "Why, dearest, why? What is the matter?"

"It is over," I murmured incoherently, "leave me. I do not wish to speak to you any more.

I do not wish to marry you. I want to go away and never see you again.''

''Mura! you are dreaming, you are out of your mind! What have I done that you should speak to me like this?''

His bewilderment and despair only irritated me the more. ''You will drag me to ruin and misfortune. I was told so; and I know, I feel that it is true.''

''You were told so?'' gasped Paul. ''What are you saying? Mura, come to your senses. Who has put such preposterous notions into your head?''

Notwithstanding my dazed and drugged state of mind, I felt that to tell him about the fortune-teller would neither convince nor impress him; he would probably laugh, and try to coax or scold me back to my senses. So I wrapped myself in an obstinate and mysterious silence.

The unhappy man was perplexed and distressed.

''Who has poisoned your mind against me, Mura? Think, think a moment; who in all the world could love you more than I do? Who could protect you and care for you better than I can, poor helpless creature that you are?''

But I was possessed by the blind obstinacy of

madness. *Quem Deus vult perdere, prius de-*
mentat. My destiny was coming upon me at the
very time I thought to evade it.

"Let me be!" My hands twisted themselves
from his grasp. "I will not see you again! I
will not!"

"But I will," cried Kamarowsky, clasping my
wrist in an iron grip, and his long, languorous eyes
opened wide and flamed into mine. "Do you
think that because I am kind and patient you can
play fast and loose with me? No indeed, no indeed; you have promised to be mine, and I shall
make you keep your word."

Never had I seen him like this nor dreamed that
he could be so fierce and resolute. I felt dizzy
and bewildered. I felt the bats of madness flying
in my brain. I raised my eyes with a scornful
smile to his: how could he keep me against my
will?

As if he had divined my thought he bent forward with his passionate face close to mine. "Do
not think you can escape me," he said. "Do not
imagine it for a moment. Mura, I know you well.
You need to be mastered, and I shall master you.
As long as I live, remember—as long as I live you
shall not escape me."

These words seemed to pierce my dizzy brain

like red-hot needles. "As long as he lives I shall not escape him. *As long as he lives—!*"

I raised my eyes and looked at him; then I drooped my lashes—and smiled.

The subtle cunning of madness stirred within me.

XXXI

PAUL KAMAROWSKY appeared not to notice it. He continued to speak agitatedly, holding my unwilling hand in his.

"I know, Mura, that you have done many unworthy things in the course of your life; I know that you are not what I would have you be; but my pity for your misfortunes is far greater than my resentment at your faults. I know that you are ill; I know that you have had none but rakes and reprobates around you; it shall be my duty to strengthen you and uphold you with my love. I will help you, Mura, whether you wish it or not; I will save you in spite of yourself."

Ah, miserable creature that I was, why did I not throw myself upon his mercy and confide my doubts and my despair to his generous heart? Why did I not surrender my poor sick soul to his keeping? This was indeed the last time that salvation opened its haven to my shipwrecked soul; but I knew it not, and like a boat adrift in the darkness I swept on towards the storm.

He continued to speak. "If I have not wanted

to know about your past, it has not been from
cowardice nor from the fear of any man; but from
distrust of my own heart, Mura, for fear lest my
love for you should wane. Whereas it is my duty
and my mission to love you, Marie Nicolaevna, to
love and save you from your own weakness and
the iniquity of the world. You are still so young
—hardly less of a child than little Tioka—notwithstanding the storms of passion and sin that have
passed over your head. All you need is to live
among right-minded people who will love you. I
shall love you, Mura; and my mother, gentle soul
that she is, will take you to her heart; and so will
my sisters. Then when you find yourself surrounded by such pure, kind and simple affections,
you, too, will become simple, kind and pure again.''

His voice broke. ''We shall be so happy; and
Tioka and Grania will be happy; and so will your
good old father. He shall come and live with us.
How is it you never think of your father, Mura?
The generous, broken-hearted old man in that des-
olate house of Otrada?''

Hot tears rushed to my eyes. My father!
My stately father, with his venerable white hair,
and his proud blue eyes—the ''terrible O'Rourke,''
living in that deserted house, widowed, desolate
and alone. There was no one to coax him out of

his grief or his anger; no arms went round his neck, no laughing voices cried to him: "Father, don't be the terrible O'Rourke!" I covered my face with my hands.

Kamarowsky bent over me. "Is it not wickedness, Mura, to throw away one's life as you do? To rush from place to place, from emotion to emotion, from misery to despair? Is it not more than wickedness—is it not madness?"

"Madness!" As if the word had rent a veil before my eyes, I looked my calamity full in the face. Yes, it was madness; it was the hereditary curse of my mother's people. I was like my mother's two wild-faced, frenzied sisters, whom we used to run away from and laugh at when we were children, Olga and I. . . . Madness! In my delicate blue veins it had taken root again, and now its monstrous flower opened its crashing petals in my brain. I was mad, there was no doubt of it and no help for it. *I was mad.*

I spoke the words softly to myself, and the very sound of them made me laugh. It amused me to think that no one knew my thoughts. I felt like a naughty little girl hiding in a dark cupboard while everybody is looking for her. The dark cupboard was my mind, and I had discovered madness there.

Undoubtedly I was bereft of reason; and my mother's sisters, now for so many years entombed in an asylum at Warsaw, were assuredly not more mad than I. The thought of this, also, made me laugh. I whispered to myself: "I am cleverer than they. I am as mad as they are, but no one shall ever know it!"

I have no other explanation to give, no other justification. I was demented, and I knew it. Sometimes in the night I started up wide awake, and the horror of the thought that I was alone with myself—with myself who was mad!—froze me into a statue of ice. As soon as I could stir a limb I would creep from my bed, steal out into the silent corridors of the hotel, and run with chattering teeth along the red-carpeted passages between the long double rows of boots, which to my eyes appeared like little monsters crouching at the thresholds; then up the great staircase, turning round every moment to look behind me, until I reached the fourth floor and the room of Elise and the children.

Softly I would tap at the door, and call:— "Elise!"

"Yes, madame." Elise Perrier always answered immediately, as if she never slept.

"Elise, I want you."

"Yes, madame, I shall come at once," and I could hear her rising from her bed.

Then I ran back through the silent corridors, and when I passed Count Kamarowsky's door I trembled and shuddered and felt constrained to stop. I looked at his yellow boots—square and placid, with their mouths open and their tongues hanging out—and I experienced a wild sensation of fear and loathing for him and for them.

I made a grimace at those hateful boots and hurried away to shut myself in my room and await Elise.

She would come in, pale and tidy in her red woolen dressing-gown, with a little cap on her head. She sat down quietly by my bedside and held my hand. Sometimes she read aloud to me; sometimes she repeated Swiss poems and ballads that she remembered from her schooldays; and I soon grew calm again as I listened to her quiet voice and felt the clasp of her small roughened hand on mine.

Gradually a sort of frenzied fear of Kamarowsky took possession of me. I was obsessed continuously with the idea that I must escape from him at all costs, or die. My every fiber shrank at the slightest touch of his hand. I longed never to see him again. I longed to know that the world held him no more. It was a blind instinctive frenzy that I endured without reasoning about it. My constant and only preoccupation was to fly from him who spelt ruin, and to cling to Naumoff, my deliverer.

"Nicolas Naumoff! Nicolas Naumoff!" I repeated his name all day long like a kind of exorcism against Kamarowsky; sometimes I felt as if I were stifled, as if I must hold my breath until he was near.

On his side, Naumoff, who frequently came to see us, was reserved and shy, and did not venture to believe in what nevertheless he could not but read in my eyes. Knowing nothing of my insensate notion about the diviner's prophecy, and having no conception that to my fancy he was a rescuer sent to me by Providence, he thought I was making fun of him; or at other times he believed my predilection for him was merely the caprice of a frivolous creature accustomed to gratify every passing whim. So he held back, aggrieved and mistrustful.

And the more he held back the more was I impelled to pursue him, to hold and to vanquish him. The passionate gravity of his youthful face delighted me; I was thirsty for the unknown recesses of his soul as for a spring filled with mysterious sweetness. His voice perturbed me; his silence lashed my nerves; I lived in a perpetual quiver of rhapsodic sensibility.

I was in this frame of mind when Kamarowsky resolved to invite all his friends in Orel to a banquet in order to announce to them our imminent marriage.

At this banquet Naumoff also was present. Doubtless he already knew the announcement that his friend was going to make, yet when the Count rose to speak and laid his hand with a placid air of ownership upon mine, I saw Nicolas Naumoff turn pale. I watched with deep emotion the color slowly receding from his face; in its pallor his youthful countenance appeared to me still more beautiful; he looked indeed like the supreme deliverer—the angel of death.

I did not comprehend a word of Paul Kamarowsky's speech; I know that when it was ended he turned to me and placed a magnificent diamond ring upon my finger, and every one applauded and cheered.

Then the guests rose in turn to congratulate Kamarowsky, and to kiss my hand and wish me joy; and I know that I smiled and thanked them.

Naumoff alone had not left his place, but in the

gay chatter and stir that surrounded us no one noticed it. He soon went away; he disappeared without taking leave of any one.

Toasts and speeches followed. The waiters came and went, carrying fruits and wines and sometimes leaving the large double doors of our dining-room open behind them.

Suddenly as I raised my eyes I saw a man standing on the threshold and gazing in at us.

It was Prilukoff.

XXXII

In truth I do not know whether I felt dismayed
or glad. It was as if I were in a dream.

Since I had begun to take cocaine again, that
twilight sensation of unreality had descended anew
like a misty veil upon all my perceptions.

I could not distinguish facts from illusions.
Prilukoff had immediately disappeared—or had I
only fancied that I saw him?

Trembling a little, I rose from my place, and
while many of the guests were still talking and
laughing with their host I excused myself on the
plea of fatigue. They toasted me a last time, and
Kamarowsky kissed me ceremoniously before them
all.

With cheeks and heart aflame I hurried to my
apartments, glad to think that I should find them
dark and silent. My temples were throbbing, the
coronet of diamonds—a gift of Kamarowsky's—
weighed heavy on my brow, and my eyes seemed
to be pierced with red-hot needles.

I opened the door of my sitting-room, where a
lamp, turned low, glimmered like a star veiled in

red vapor. Behind it I could see yawning blackly the open door leading to my bedroom, which was in complete darkness.

I had a strange feeling that I was not alone. Some one was in the room—some one whom I could not discern was near to me.

Yes, a footstep approached; a strong arm encircled me. Nicolas Naumoff's voice spoke in thrilling accents: "Marie! Marie! My heart is breaking."

With a sigh of infinite weariness merging into a sense of infinite repose I laid my head against his breast. I longed to die. I felt as if I had nothing more to ask for, nothing more to desire.

But the anguish that was passing from my soul seemed to have entered into his.

"You must not marry that man! You must not, you shall not!" He gripped my shoulders as if he would crush them. "Tell me, tell me that you do not love him."

At that instant on the black background of my bedroom there appeared a form—Prilukoff! Erect in the doorway he stood watching us. Naumoff had his back to him, but across his shoulder I looked Prilukoff in the face, only a few steps from me.

My heart stood still. What would he do?

Knowing as I did his ungovernable frenzies of jealousy, his madness, his recklessness, I wondered whether he would leap forward and spring at Naumoff's throat? Would there be blows and groans and a death-struggle in my tranquil, shadowy room? Would there be a turmoil and a scandal, during which the bond of infamy that tied me to Prilukoff would be revealed to Naumoff? Revealed to Kamarowsky and to the world?

The fear of tragedy and disgrace kept me stark and terror-stricken, rooted to the spot. Then I saw Prilukoff move. Slowly he raised his right arm. His right hand clutched something which I could not see. Suddenly—incredible sight!—I saw him open his mouth wide; and never, never have I seen anything more grotesque and terrifying than that figure in the darkness with mouth gaping wide. . . .

But still his right arm moved, rising slowly and relentlessly until it was on a level with that terrible open mouth. What did the hand hold? Did I not see a gleam of polished metal?

I tried to scream, but no sound issued from my parched throat. I could see the whites of his staring upturned eyes, and the hand now motionless just in front of the open mouth—

From my throat came a hoarse whisper: ''Don't, for heaven's sake! Wait—''

Naumoff, in amazement at these words which he believed to be addressed to himself, relaxed his hold. ''What is it?'' he whispered. ''Is any one there?''

Step by step I drew back from him, with my fascinated eyes still fixed upon Prilukoff, who stood motionless as a statue in the same dreadful attitude.

''Is any one there?'' repeated Naumoff.

''Yes. Don't move.'' The words formed themselves soundlessly on my lips, but Naumoff understood them and obeyed. He neither turned nor moved.

''Stand as you are,'' I breathed; ''do not stir.'' And I glided snake-like from him.

Then with the quickness of lightning I darted upon Prilukoff, thrusting him back into the dark bedroom, clutching him by the wrist, and covering his rapid breathing with my hand. The carpet deadened our footsteps. With my elbow I pushed the door and, as it closed behind me, I turned and shot the bolt. I was locked in my room with Prilukoff.

''Hush, hush!'' I whispered, my lips almost touching his face. ''I implore you, I implore you! Do not betray me. Do not let them hear you."

Through his closed and stifled lips there issued hideous, incoherent words of vituperation.

"Hush! hush! hush!" I pressed my hand still tighter to his lips. "Forgive me! Spare me! I am yours, yours only! Donat, forgive me and keep silence!"

"Mine, mine only," breathed Prilukoff, hoarsely; "you swear it!"

"Yes! oh, yes!"

I could hear Naumoff trying the handle on the other side of the door.

"Marie! Marie! What are you doing? Why have you run away?"

Prilukoff's right hand was still uplifted, and now he held it close to his temple. As I clutched that hand I could also feel the cold contact with the steel of a revolver.

"Do you swear that you will be mine forever?"

I murmured something inarticulate. Naumoff was calling under his breath: "Marie! Marie! Open the door."

Prilukoff raised his voice slightly. "Swear to me that you loathe that man and the other; swear that if I murdered them both you would still be mine."

"Yes, yes. Speak softly!"

"Swear it! Swear that they shall both die, that you will help me to rid the world of them. Swear it." I could feel his hand tenser against his temple, I could feel the first finger crooking itself over the trigger. "Unless you swear," hissed Prilukoff, "I shall shoot myself here, this instant."

I did so. He repeated the words softly with me: *"I swear—that—they shall die."* And something within me kept saying: "I am dreaming all this."

"That is not enough!" breathed Prilukoff. "Swear it on the life of Tioka."

My parched lips opened, but the iniquitous words would not pass my throat.

Then Prilukoff pushed me from him and the fingers of his right hand moved. I heard a slight clicking sound. I threw myself forward.

"I swear it—"

And I swore it on the life of Tioka.

Prilukoff's hand dropped to his side; he seemed to reel slightly, and staggering backwards leaned against the foot of my bed.

Naumoff on the other side of the door was growing impatient. He shook the handle.

I bent over to Prilukoff. "Are you going to

betray me? If I open this door, will you show yourself?"

He laughed derisively. "Go along, go along," he muttered. And I opened the door.

"Why did you run away?" asked Naumoff, taking my hand.

I closed the door behind me. I felt no more fear of Prilukoff. I felt no more fear of any one or anything. My heart seemed turned to stone. And as I stood thus, some one else knocked at the outside door. It was Kamarowsky.

And the door was not locked! I turned quickly and blew out the lamp.

But Naumoff had taken a rapid step forward, and turned the key in the lock. Then he stood still, leaning against the door.

Kamarowsky outside heard him; and thinking it was I, murmured softly: "Good-night! Good-night, my darling!"

Then I was seized with a convulsive fit of laughter. I laughed and laughed, shaken from head to foot by a wild paroxysm of mirth. I could not leave off laughing. I laughed until the laughter became a spasm which racked and agonized me; my teeth chattered, I trembled and quaked; and still the hysterical laughter continued, shaking my entire frame as an aspen is shaken by a brutal hand. I laughed and laughed, trying to laugh softly in order that those three men standing in the dark should not hear me.

The thought of the three men motionless behind the doors made me laugh more than ever. Tears ran down my face, my head felt as if it would burst asunder. And still I rocked in the throes of frantic laughter until body and soul seemed to be shattered and rent. . . .

I staggered and sank to the floor.

Naumoff bent over me. I felt his icy hands passing over my face. Then we remained quite silent in the dark.

Slowly, reluctantly Kamarowsky's footsteps had passed away down the corridor. . . .

I mustered strength enough to whisper to Naumoff: "Go—send Elise to me—quickly!"

Naumoff obeyed.

Yes, Nicolas Naumoff—submissive soul!—has always obeyed.

XXXIII

I was ill in bed for a long time. I lay supine and motionless, feeling—as once, long before—as if I were lying at the bottom of a well. In the distance, far above me, life and the world went whirling on; but nothing in me or of me stirred, except that at every pulse-beat my life-blood seemed to be gently, inexorably ebbing away. The doctors bent over me with anxious faces; on my body I felt the burning weight of ice; my arteries contracted under the grip of ergot and chloride of iron. Still slowly and inexorably I glided, as on a smooth and shallow river, towards death.

Tioka and Grania had been sent to stay with friends in Kharkov.

Naumoff came every day to ask for news, and sent me flowers; but he was never allowed to see me. Kamarowsky had permission to come into my room for ten minutes every morning, but he was not allowed to speak to me.

Prilukoff, locked in my rooms, watched over me night and day.

Nobody knew of his existence, for no one was allowed to enter my apartment. How and when he slept and took his meals I do not know. Perhaps Elise looked after that. He undoubtedly grew thinner, more haggard and spectral every day with sleeplessness, fasting and anxiety.

Night and day he sat at my bedside watching me. Sometimes, as I lay prostrate with closed eyes, I said to myself that I must open them and look at him; but so great seemed the effort of raising my heavy eyelids, that frequently hours passed and I could not do so. When at last I lifted my leaden lashes, I saw him, always sitting motionless beside me with his gaze fixed on my face. With renewed effort I faintly contracted the muscles of my face and attempted to smile at him. Then, worn out with fatigue, I dropped my heavy lids and my soul floated away again towards unconsciousness. . . .

When I began to get better I noticed to my amazement that Prilukoff talked to himself all the time. Perhaps he had done so from the first, but then I was too weak to understand or even to hear him. Now that a little strength was coming back to me each day, I could hear and comprehend the words he uttered; it was a succession of imprecations, of incoherent and disconnected maledictions hurled against Naumoff and Kamarowsky, who as he thought had snatched my heart from him, and would be the ruin and the death of me. I could hear him murmuring:

"They must be got rid of; we have sworn it. They must die."

Towards evening his meager face grew red as if with fever, and his mutterings increased, became more rapid and excited. He would bend over me with his nightmare face as I lay weak and helpless on my pillows.

"They are outside there, in the corridor, both of them. I can hear them walking up and down, whispering together—talking about you. But they are doomed, are they not? Irrevocably doomed. You have sworn it. Tell me that it is so."

I faltered "Yes," hoping to silence him, but he never ceased his uncanny mutterings; and the idea of murder completely possessed his disordered brain. Elise, moving like a little frightened ghost through the locked and darkened rooms, frequently attempted to come to my aid.

"Go away; leave her alone," she would say to Prilukoff. "Do you want her to fall ill again? Why don't you go to sleep? Why don't you eat? Why don't you go out?"

But Prilukoff stared at her with vacant eyes, then went into the dining-room and drank some vodka, and soon he was bending over me again.

"Mind, I am not going to do it alone," he whispered, "so that afterwards you would be afraid and horrified of me. No, no. You shall help me. You shall attend to one, and I to the other."

By degrees, as strength returned to me and dispelled the torpor that had numbed my brain, I understood Prilukoff's ravings, and was aghast at them. Absorbed in his monstrous dream, he delighted in planning all the details of the double crime.

"What I want is to be alone with the man I saw holding you in his arms the other evening." He ground his teeth. "As for your betrothed, you shall give him a dose of curare or atropine. An exquisite wedding cup for the bridegroom!"

Then I burst into tears of terror and weakness, while the indignant Elise, hastening to my aid, would grasp Prilukoff's arm and compel him to leave me. He would sit gloomily in a corner, or go into the adjoining room, but a little while afterwards he was there again, raving as before.

"Elise," I whispered to her one evening, "I am afraid, I am terribly afraid of him."

"Shall I tell some one about it? Shall I tell Monsieur the Count?" exclaimed Elise.

"No, no," I cried.

"Might I—might I tell Monsieur Naumoff?"

I hesitated; but when I recalled those golden eyes that turned to me filled with such trust and adoration I shook my head. "No, tell no one, Elise, tell no one." And I hid my face in the pillows.

At last a day came when I was able to be up for an hour, and it was no longer possible to prevent Kamarowsky from coming to see me. Prilukoff refused to go away; I could not get him to stir from my room. At last, having compelled me to repeat the abominable vow, having forced me to invoke once more the seraphic image of little Tioka as tutelar genius of a monstrous crime, he went away, passing through my dressing-room to an outer passage at the back of the hotel.

Elise dressed me and placed me in an armchair near the window, where I reclined, trembling and weak. Then I sent word to Count Kamarowsky that I would see him.

He came in full of emotion and joy. "At last, at last you are better," he cried, his kind eyes alight with pleasure. "But how pale you are, how dreadfully pale." And bending over me, he kissed my hair with infinite tenderness.

As I saw him standing before me, smiling and well, the murderous ravings of Prilukoff and my own iniquitous vow seemed but a figment of

my morbid fancy, a half-forgotten illusion of my
delirium, dissolving and fading away like a dark
dream at daylight.

Kamarowsky held my hand tightly clasped in
his, as if he were half afraid I might vanish from
him. "What a poor little blue-white hand!" he
said. "You have become quite transparent,
Mura; I think I can look right through you and
see your soul, trembling and flickering like a little
flame!"

I smiled at him. All my morbid fear and dis-
like of him, even as all my sudden insensate
infatuation for Naumoff, was spent. Nothing
remained of the storm my soul and senses had
passed through but a limitless weakness and
languor. I yearned to rest, to sleep, to sink out
of life and be no more. . . .

A few moments later they announced Naumoff,
who had brought me some roses. I was neither
glad nor sorry to see him. Punctually when an
hour had elapsed Elise Perrier sent my visitors
away and put me to bed again.

I fell asleep almost immediately.

When I reopened my eyes, twilight filled my
room with shadows and there was Prilukoff,
sitting beside my bed, talking to himself about
murder, revenge and poison.

XXXIV

Every day my fear of Prilukoff increased. I had only one thought—to escape from him, to go far away where he could never find me; better still, to hide with Tioka and Elise in some distant spot, where neither this terrible maniac nor yet Naumoff, nor even Kamarowsky, could ever reach me.

I thought of Otrada, my home. But how could my unhappy father protect me against the loving persistence of Kamarowsky, against Naumoff's passionate daring, or Prilukoff's diabolic designs?

In the rare moments when I was alone with Elise, we talked it over. In trembling whispers, glancing constantly round lest the Scorpion should be on the watch, we concerted the manner of our flight.

We made a thousand different plans, all equally extravagant and impracticable. In our luxurious hotel rooms we were imprisoned like mice in a trap. We never opened a door without finding a maid awaiting our orders, or a zealous and obsequious waiter bowing to us, or Kamarowsky asking for news, or Naumoff waiting with a bunch of flowers in his hand.

We closed the door, and found ourselves shut up with Prilukoff, ferocious and maniacal, who glowered at us with the eye of a tiger.

A thousand times in my weakness and despair I was on the point of throwing the door wide open and calling for help—calling Kamarowsky and Naumoff, and crying to them: "Look! a man is shut up in here. For days and days he has been torturing and threatening me. The man is a criminal and a thief, and he has been my lover. Save me from him!"

But then I pictured to myself the scene of violence that would follow, the room echoing with revolver shots; and at the mere thought of it, in my weak and exhausted state, I fell into long fainting fits from which Elise had the greatest difficulty in reviving me.

One morning Elise had an idea: "Let us confide in the doctor."

I agreed. But the thought agitated me so that when the doctor came he found me trembling, with a rapid, irregular pulse and panting breath.

"Doctor—" I began.

"Ah, but this is bad, very bad. What is the

meaning of all this agitation? Did you sit up too long? If you are not a better patient, I shall have to complain of you to my friend Paul.''

His friend Paul! True. He was a friend, an intimate friend, of Kamarowsky's. How could I ever have had the idea that he would keep our secret, that he would not betray my intended flight? It was a crazy notion of Elise's. I cast a significant glance at her, and was silent.

He prescribed bromides and recommended absolute rest of body and mind. Scarcely was he gone when to my astonishment the long curtain that hung in front of an alcove where Elise kept my dresses moved slightly. Then they parted, and Prilukoff appeared.

Ah! he had not gone out as he had pretended when the doctor had been announced! He had hidden himself. What if I had spoken?

My fear of him turned to frenzy: I thought him endowed with supernatural powers. My room seemed to be filled with innumerable Prilukoffs peering out at me from every corner. I clung to Elise. ''We must go away, we must go away to-morrow,'' I whispered. ''Do you understand?''

''Yes, madame,'' was Elise's firm and humble reply.

"Send to fetch little Tioka; send for him at once."

"Yes, madame."

Later, while she was dressing me, she stooped to draw on my stocking—Prilukoff was reading in the adjoining room—and she murmured:

"We have no money to travel with."

"You must ask Count Kamarowsky for some; he will give you all we want," I whispered.

"Not without asking what it is for. We shall need a great deal."

"Oh, Elise, think, think of something," I sighed, and felt myself turning faint.

"What are you two mumbling and plotting?" growled Prilukoff's voice from the adjoining room.

We were silent.

Tenderly and anxiously assisted by Kamarowsky and Elise I went down to the terrace that day, and spent the afternoon reclining on a couch in the mild spring sunshine, with eyes closed and every limb relaxed. I thought of our impending flight. Kamarowsky, seated beside me, kept silence, thinking I was asleep.

Shortly afterwards I heard Tioka's quick little footsteps running across the terrace towards us. Kamarowsky doubtless warned him to keep very quiet, for I heard him stepping nearer on tip-toe, and without a word he clambered on to Kamarowsky's knee and laid his fair head confidingly against his shoulder.

Beneath my drooping lashes, I gazed at them, and thought of the hideous plot that was weaving itself round this kind and generous man, who all unknowing pressed forward towards treachery and death; and I thought of the iniquitous oath which had placed a circlet of blood round that fair childish head.

With a sob I raised myself and stretched out my arms to them both.

.   .   .   .

It was eleven o'clock on the following night. Elise put out the lights and prepared the bromide and water on my little table. Prilukoff was rambling backwards and forwards between bedroom and drawing-room, smoking a cigarette.

"Elise," I whispered. "Are we ready?"

Elise nodded.

"Elise, when? When is it to be?"

"Hush, madame. Later on, towards morning; as soon"—with her head she indicated Prilukoff —"as soon as he is asleep."

"But he never sleeps, Elise!"

Elise looked at me. "He will sleep to-night," she said; and there was an icy hardness in her tone that I had never heard before.

"Why will he sleep? How can you know?"

Before she could answer, Prilukoff reappeared in the doorway. He had a glass of vodka in his hand.

"This accursed throat!" he said, throwing his cigarette away and putting his hand to his neck. "Everything I swallow burns and scratches me." He coughed and cleared his throat. "You can go, Elise. I shall see to anything your mistress needs."

Elise did not reply. With a hard, pinched face she poured the water into my glass and dropped two little bromide tablets into it. Then with her back turned to Prilukoff she fixed her eyes upon me and moved her lips: *"Do not drink."* She formulated the words clearly but without sound. I stared at her in bewilderment, and she made the movement with her lips again: *"Do not drink anything."* Then seeing that, notwithstanding my astonishment, I had understood her, she said respectfully: "Good night, madame," and left the room.

She went out by the bath-room door, of which she always kept the key.

Prilukoff dropped into an armchair and yawned. "This accursed throat," he repeated.

He poured out a glass of water from the crystal carafe on my table and swallowed it at a gulp. Then he coughed violently.

"The devil!" he exclaimed. "This too! It tastes like some beastly concoction of—of chloral." He coughed and yawned again. Then he leaned his head against my bed. A few moments later he started up.

"The devil!" he repeated, rising to his feet. I saw him go to the little table on which Elise every evening left some coffee ready on a spirit lamp; he lit it, and I dreamily watched the thin blue waverings of the flame. While the coffee was heating Prilukoff constantly cleared his throat, with the same murmured oath. Now he poured the smoking coffee into a cup and sipped it. "By all the infernal powers—" he cried, and turned suddenly to look at me.

I did not dare to shut my eyes, much as I should have liked to do so. He came up to my bed and bending over me looked me in the face. Then he touched my shoulder.

"See here!"

I drooped my eyelids drowsily. "Yes, dear! What is it?"

"Just taste this coffee," and he pushed the cup against my lips.

I sat up and with a smile took the cup from his hands.

"It burns," I said, barely touching it with my lips and making a little grimace.

"Drink it!" he roared in a terrible voice, though his eyes were half shut as if he could not keep awake.

I took a sip of the coffee: it scraped my throat like a rake. I thought of Elise and understood. For a moment the idea flashed through my brain to say that I found nothing the matter with it. Then I changed my mind.

"Good heavens!" I exclaimed. "What have they put in this coffee? It tastes like poison!"

Prilukoff bent still closer over me.

"If you had said it was all right, I should have strangled you."

My teeth chattered, partly through the taste of the chloral, partly through my fear of Prilukoff.

"Have you drunk much of it?" I gasped. "You ought to call for help."

But Prilukoff had sunk into an armchair, and already, with his head rolled back and his mouth open, he slept.

XXXV

How did we three hapless, terrified creatures manage to escape from the hotel that night?

Tioka, wakened out of his sleep at three o'clock, kept on whimpering.

"Where are we going? I am afraid. I want Papa Paul! Call Papa Paul."

As we descended the dark staircase a night porter, dozing in the hall, started up and came towards us, blinking and yawning. When he caught sight of Elise, laden with shawls and medicine bottles—which constituted all our luggage—he seemed greatly astonished.

For a moment no one spoke. Then: "I am feeling ill," I said. "We are going to the doctor. Please call a carriage for me."

"But excuse me, madame," stammered the man. "Had I not better telephone to the doctor to come to the hotel?" His eyes wandered suspiciously from me to the lachrymose Tioka, and from Tioka to Elise and her burdens.

"Open the door," said Elise authoritatively, "and call a carriage, at once."

The man shook his head.

239

Then I saw Elise gather all the shawls into a heap on her left arm, as with her right hand she searched for something under her cloak. She drew out a crumpled piece of paper, and with a gesture of solemn deliberation she proffered it to the man. It was a banknote of a hundred rubles.

The man took the note, stared at it, and turned it round and round in his fingers. Then he raised his eyes and gazed in stupefaction at Elise.

"Open that door and call a carriage," commanded Elise, in a thin voice.

The man obeyed. As the large door swung back we could see that it was nearly dawn; the sound of distant church bells came to us across the clear, keen air. Elise raised her hand to her forehead and made the sign of the cross. . . . She had plundered the white elephant!

Oh, Elise Perrier, not least among my great pangs of remorse is the thought that I have dragged you down into my own dishonor. For me and through me, your honest hard-working hand and your innocent soul were stained with guilt.

While we stood waiting for the man to return, I thought I heard a door open and close overhead.

I started. "Could it be Prilukoff?" I gasped to Elise.

She shook her head.

"Elise, what have you done to him?"

"I put chloral into everything—into everything," and Elise shuddered.

"Oh, Elise! What if he were to die?"

She made no answer.

"And if we were to be sent to prison?"

The bells were ringing joyfully in the limpid Easter dawn.

Elise closed her eyes, and her lips moved: "Dear God of Eastertide, give us Thy blessing."

Tioka stopped crying to look at her. Then with an enchanting smile he did as she had done. He closed his blue eyes, which were still full of tears, and said: "Dear God of Eastertide, give us Thy blessing."

The days swung forward.

Prilukoff was the first to discover us. We had been hidden in Vienna, in the little Hotel Victoria, less than a week, when one morning he stood before our terror-stricken eyes.

He was derisive and sarcastic; but finding us alone—without Kamarowsky, without Naumoff—the maleficent frenzy that possessed him at Orel seemed to have vanished. He was soon quite genial and good-humored; he was once more the

Prilukoff we had known at Moscow, the trusty knight—Elise's Lohengrin!

He did not speak of the past; he made no allusion to the chloral. Neither did he ever recall his murderous purposes; and sometimes I thought that I had dreamt it all. Cheerful and light-hearted, he took us out for drives in carriages and motors, to the Prater, to the Brühl, to the Semmering; he insisted upon our going with him to theaters, concerts and cabarets.

And to pay for it all we had recourse to the black leather satchel. When any money was required, we found it there. No accounts were kept. Simply, and as a matter of course, we dipped into the lacerated body of the white elephant and took what we needed.

I let myself drift with the tide; I gave no thought either to the future or the past, but yielded myself passively to my fate like a straw afloat on the water. . . .

One day I saw in the newspapers that Kamarowsky was putting in motion the police of every city in Europe in his efforts to find me. Then, on Prilukoff's advice, I sent Elise to Neuchâtel to telegraph to him from there in my name, in order to tranquilize him and mislead his inquiries.

No sooner was the name of Kamarowsky men-

tioned between us than Prilukoff became sullen
and gloomy again. He sulked and glowered at
me, and passed the whole day without speaking a
word.

On this particular day we had taken a box at
the *Theater An der Wien*, having promised Tioka
that he should hear "The Merry Widow." Long
before it was time to go, the little fellow was
dressed and ready, jumping up and down in front
of the window.

"Let us make haste," he cried. "The carriage
will be tired of waiting. Let us make haste!"

Suddenly he uttered a shriek of joy. "Mother,
mother, look! There is Papa Paul! I can see
him—he has just passed. Papa Paul!" he
shouted with all his might.

Prilukoff caught him by his little jacket and
drew him roughly from the window. Then he
himself looked out.

"Sure enough," he said, shutting the window
and looking at me with that terrible crooked smile
I had learned to dread. "It is Kamarowsky."

There was a moment's silence. Then he said:
"And now I have had enough of this. We will
end it." Murder gleamed in his eyes.

I clasped Tioka in my arms—the child was quite
sad and hurt by Prilukoff's sudden rudeness—and

as I kissed his soft curls I breathed Elise's prayer: "Dear God of Eastertide, give us Thy blessing."

But alas! it was Easter no longer.

In spite of what had happened, we went to the theater that night. And there, while the music swayed us in the undulating rhythm of the waltz, and little Tioka gazed enraptured at the stage, Prilukoff, sitting behind me in the shadow, formulated his plans for the crime.

"You have sworn it on your child, remember. If you break your oath, he will be the sufferer."

Tioka turned to us with shrill laughter. "Oh, look, mama, how beautiful it all is! Look at that fat policeman dancing."

"When Kamarowsky finds you here—" Prilukoff went on; but I interrupted him.

"No, no. Let us leave Vienna at once."

"It is useless. He will find us all the same. You are too striking," he added, "to pass unobserved." And with a cynical laugh he surveyed me from head to foot. "He had better not find me with you. I shall remain at the Hotel Victoria; but you and Tioka must go to the Bristol, and when that man joins you, this is what you must do—"

His iniquitous suggestions floated on the buoyant waltz music like carrion on the surface of a sparkling stream.

I shuddered in horror. "No, no," I murmured. "Have pity! No . . . no!"

Oh! that music of Lehar's, that every one knows and every one whistles, and that is played by every organ at every street-corner—what monstrous secrets does it murmur to my heart!

Ich gehe zu Maxim,
Da bin ich sehr intim . . .

The joyous verses ring in my ears like the shrieks of maleficent Furies, scourging me with nefarious counsels and diabolic commands. . . .

And while little Tioka laughs and claps his hands, I, his mother, sink ever deeper and deeper into the gulf of despair; and crime, like a sea of mire, closes its corrupt waves over my head.

XXXVI

Everything came about as Prilukoff had foreseen. Kamarowsky found me the following evening alone with Tioka at the Bristol Hotel. He overwhelmed me with reproaches and with endearments.

I maintained a mysterious silence, which he interpreted merely as the caprice of a spoiled child; nor did he take umbrage at it. He was too happy at having found me to care to quarrel either with the Fates or with me. All he said was: "Marie, I shall not leave you again." And the promise sounded almost like a threat.

For some time Prilukoff gave no sign. I might have thought he had forgotten me. He had fixed a definitive space of time: ten days.

On the eighth day he sent me a note, telling me to come to the Hotel Victoria that evening at nine o'clock. He would then provide we with what was needful. I was not to fail—or he would come himself.

I dined with Paul Kamarowsky as usual; then, pleading a headache, I retired to my room at eight o'clock.

Half an hour later a closed carriage was conveying me to the Hotel Victoria.

From Prilukoff's hands I received a syringe, two tiny bottles, and a box filled with globules of curare, nitrate of amyl and chloroform. From his set gray lips I received instructions how to use these things. His teeth were chattering as well as my own; his hands were ice-cold and his eyes distraught.

Then I fell on my knees at his feet. I implored him with all the strength of desperation to forego his abominable purpose. I reminded him of his past, of his unsullied youth, of the kind and generous love that had at first bound him to me; with tears streaming down my face I clung to his knees and swore to him eternal gratitude, eternal devotion, if only he would not stain my soul with crime, if only he would not ruin himself forever with so dark and vile a deed.

I beat my forehead against his feet, entreating of him death for myself, but pity, pity for a generous, chivalrous man whose only wish was to protect and save me.

What heaven-inspired words were granted me that I was able to move him? I cannot tell; but suddenly a great shudder went through him and agonized sobs shook his frame. He bent down and raised me. Then he sank into an armchair and wept aloud with uplifted face, a terrible spectacle of anguish and desolation.

I also wept, kneeling beside him, kissing his hands, thanking him, blessing him.

"Donat, dearest, do not weep! It has been all a dream—a fearful dream. We were ill—we were poor demented creatures. God will not remember it—He will cancel and forgive everything. Let us thank Him, Donat, for not permitting us to do harm to any one. Let us begin life all over again —a new, honorable life."

"Ah, no," groaned Prilukoff. "I am a criminal. I have stolen!"

"Never mind, never mind. You will give it all back. I will help you to give it all back. We must be prepared to face suffering and humiliation, but we shall atone; we shall take up our lives again, and retrieve and redeem the past."

Even while I spoke I resolved that I would confess everything to Kamarowsky, and this thought filled me with joy. I would reveal to him the darkest recesses of my soul; I would confess the iniquitous treachery plotted against him, my every act of baseness and of shame. He would drive me from him in loathing, he would tread me under foot like some poisonous thing, but I would bow my head beneath his wrath and his disdain. I would go far away and live the rest of my life in humility and penitence. I would perhaps link my fate with that of Prilukoff, the degraded outcast . . . yes, my penance should be to stay forever with him who inspired me now with so much horror and fear. . . .

Carried away by an ecstasy of feeling, we knelt down in that paltry hotel-room and thanked God for having opened our eyes, for having touched our hearts, for having saved us. Then praying aloud: *"Lord, let not our sins be counted against us . . ."* we broke the syringe and the phials of poison into a thousand fragments. Prilukoff tore the flesh of his hands as he snapped the hollow steel needle, which thrust itself into his palm like some fierce, living thing. *"Blot out our transgressions and remember not our iniquities . . ."* We trampled on the globules of amyl and chloroform, setting free the lethal vapors, which turned us giddy. Intoxicated with them and with our own emotions we fell once more on our knees, praying with uplifted hands: *"Deliver us from our sins . . . of Thy mercy save us . . . save us . . ."*

XXXVII

I REMEMBER that once in our childhood we were by the sea—I cannot tell in what country we were, nor what sea it was—and our English governess took us out one morning on the beach to see a tidal wave.

"What is a tidal wave, Miss Williams?" we inquired.

"Two or three immense waves which only come once a year," replied the sibylline Miss Williams. "Now keep quiet and look."

We kept quiet and looked. And presently we thought we could see a huge wave, larger than all the others, coming towards us from the horizon.

"Look! Look there! It is the tidal wave!"

"No," said Miss Williams. "That is not it."

And, indeed, presently there appeared a wave which was greater still—it reared its crest, towered aloft, and fell.

"That was it! That was it!"

But still farther away, on the line of the horizon, a mighty wave—a veritable wall of water—was approaching, formidable, gigantic, fabulous. . . .

That was the "tidal wave."

250

In the course of my life, when events tragic and inexorable have raised their threatening billows above me and caught me in their crashing downfall, sweeping me like a piece of frail wreckage towards destruction, I have said to myself: "This is the tidal wave. Nothing worse can follow. Nothing more terrible than this can come upon me."

But lo! behind that great wave of calamity another and still greater has followed, and still another and another—fabulous waves of tragedy and disaster.

Thus it was that when I left Prilukoff that evening I thought that the tidal wave of my destiny had at last passed over me. Nothing more could crush and overwhelm me; before me stretched only the limitless levels of grief and remorse.

But it was not so. Another—the last—wave of disaster was rearing itself like the fabulous wall of water of my childhood's recollections, carrying me on its crest, crashing down with me to irremediable ruin, to the fathomless abyss of crime.

That very night Tioka fell ill. Elise came hurriedly into my room to call me. "Come at once, my lady. The young master is very ill. He is delirious and keeps talking to himself."

I ran into the child's room. He was sitting up in bed, his wide eyes glowing in his fevered face. Where and when had I once before seen him like this? . . .

His mind was wandering, and he talked incessantly—about Tania whom he had not seen or mentioned for the past two years, about his grandmother, and the old dog Bear. Then suddenly he asked for a picture and for some poetry. "Mama," he said, clinging to my neck, "say the poetry to me, the poetry—"

"What poetry, oh, my darling, my darling?"

"The poetry about the picture. Say it. Say it." He began to cry and tremble with his hot cheek close to mine.

I racked my brain for a poem:

"This is the miller who lives in the mill,
The mill beside the river, oh! . . ."

"No, no, no!" cried the child. "Not that!"
I tried again:

"Brown-eyed Peter is going for a soldier;
Going for a soldier with his little turn-up nose . . ."

"No, no, no!" shrieked Tioka despairingly. "Tania, Tania—the moon—the picture. Say it quickly!"

A lightning flash seemed to tear the clouds of

oblivion from my brain and illuminate the past.
I was once more in Vassili's country house . . .
once more I entered the dim white nursery where
my children, like two blonde seraphs, lay asleep.
. . . A lamp hanging between the two little cots
lit up an artless picture hanging on the wall—a
rippling-haired Madonna standing in a star-lit
sky, holding in her youthful arms the infant Jesus
with a count's coronet on His head.

Crying softly as I cradled my son's fair head
upon my breast, I began:

"When little children sleep, the Virgin Mary
    Steps with white feet upon the crescent moon . . ."

.   .   .   .

Tioka grew worse. With glittering eyes and
thin red cheeks he cried all day long that he
wanted Grania—that he wanted Tania. But
Grania had been sent away hurriedly for fear of
infection—Count Kamarowsky's sister had come
and taken him away—and Tania, alas! the gentle
little Tania, far away in the castle of the Tarnowskys, had doubtless long since forgotten her
brother Tioka and her heart-broken mother as
well.

The doctors shook their heads gravely as they
stood by the tumbled cot in which the little boy
tossed and moaned ceaselessly: "A train—a

train is running over my head. Take it away! It hurts me, it hurts me . . ." And as they looked into his throat, which was dark red, almost purple in hue, they murmured: "Diphtheria? Scarlet fever?" Then they went away, conversing in low tones, leaving me beside myself with grief and terror.

Kamarowsky watched with me night and day. Sometimes he fell asleep; and when I saw him sleeping, the old, unreasoning hatred for him stirred in my heart again.

Prilukoff had left the Hotel Victoria, and had taken a room at the Bristol to be near us. Occasionally I saw him for a moment standing mournful and depressed outside my door. We looked at each other with anguish-stricken eyes, but we scarcely ever spoke. I had no thought for anything but Tioka.

One night—the fourth since he had been taken ill—the child, who had been dozing for a few moments, awoke coughing and choking.

"Mother, mother!" he gasped, fixing his large frightened eyes upon me. "Why do you let me die?" Then he closed his eyes again.

I stood as if turned to stone. It was true. It was I, I who was letting him die. That idea had already flitted through my brain, but I had never dared to formulate the awful thought. As soon as he had fallen ill I had said to myself: "This is retribution. Did I not vow on Tioka's life? . . ."

I saw myself again at the theater on the evening of "The Merry Widow," and Prilukoff pointing to the child's angel head and whispering: "If you break your word, it is he who will pay for it."

Yes; Tioka was paying for it. He was paying for the iniquitous vow that had been wrung from me that night at Orel when the three men pursued me in the darkness. With his revolver pressed against his temple Prilukoff had bidden me: "Swear!" Ah, why had I not let his fate overtake him? Why had he not pulled the trigger and fallen dead at my feet? Naumoff would have rushed in, and Kamarowsky would have broken in the door, and the whole of the triple treachery and fraud and dishonor would have been revealed; but, at least, I should have been free—free to take my child and wander with him through the wide spaces of the world. Whereas, coward that I had been, the fear of disgrace had vanquished me, and the threat of ignominy and death had dragged the inhuman vow from my lips. . . . And now Tioka was paying for it.

The fierce primitive instinct of maternity awoke

within me. Weakened by illness and wakefulness, my spirit lost itself again in the dark labyrinth of superstition. My frantic gaze passed from Tioka —lying wan and wasted on his pillows, gasping like a little dying bird—to Kamarowsky stretched out in an armchair, with his flaccid hands hanging at his sides and the corners of his mouth relaxed in sleep. I looked at him; I seemed to see him for the first time—this man to save whose life I was sacrificing my own child's. Yes, Tioka was dying in order that this stranger, this outsider, this enemy might live.

When I turned towards Tioka again I saw that his eyes were open and fixed upon me. I fell on my knees beside him and whispered wildly: "Darling, darling, I will not let you die. No, my soul, my own, I will save you. You shall get well again and run out and play in the sunshine. . . . The other one shall die—but not you, not you! Now you will get well immediately. Are you not better already, my love, my own? Are you not better already?"

And my boy, cradled in my arms, smiled faintly as my soft wild whispers lulled him to sleep.

This idea now took possession of my brain, to the exclusion of all others. I thought and dreamed of nothing else. Tioka had scarlet fever and the fluctuations in his illness seemed to depend solely upon me. When I told myself that I was firmly, irrevocably resolved to compass the death of Kamarowsky, the child's fever seemed to abate, his throat was less inflamed, the pains in his head diminished. But if, as I grew calmer and clung to hope again, I hesitated in my ruthless purpose, lo! the fever seized him anew, the rushing trains went thundering over his temples, and his tender throat swelled until he could hardly draw his breath.

Prilukoff followed the oscillations of my distracted spirit with weary resignation; he was benumbed and apathetic, without mind and without will. When in the fixity of my mania I insisted upon the necessity of the crime, he would answer languidly: "Oh, no. Leave it alone. Let things be."

Then I grew more and more frenzied, weeping and tearing my hair.

"Can you not understand that Tioka is dying? Tioka, my little Tioka is dying! And it is we who are killing him."

"No, no," sighed Prilukoff. "Let things alone."

Tioka grew worse.

A day came when he could not see me or hear

me—when he lay quite still with scarcely flickering breath. Then I rose as one in a dream. I went to Prilukoff's room.

He sat listlessly by the window, smoking. I seized him by the arm.

"Donat Prilukoff, I renew my oath. Paul Kamarowsky shall die within this year!"

"All right, all right!" grumbled Prilukoff, wearied to exhaustion by my constant changes of mood. "Let us finish him once for all, and have done with it."

I gasped. "Where? When? Is it *you* who will—"

Prilukoff raised his long, languid eyes. "Whatever you like," he said. Then he added in a spent voice: "I am very tired."

And it was I who urged him, who pushed him on, who hurried him to think out and shape our plans. He was languid and inert. Sometimes he would look dully at me and say: "What a terrible woman you are." But I thought only of Tioka, and my eager and murderous frenzy increased.

And behold! Tioka got better. This chance coincidence assumed in my diseased brain the character of a direct answer from heaven. The sacrifice had been accepted!

A year later, when I stood before the judges who were to sentence me, no word of this delusion passed my lips. Demented though I was, I knew myself to be demented; I knew that this idea of a barter with heaven was an insensate idea; and yet, by some fallacy of my hallucinated brain, I believed—do I not even now believe it?—that my vow had been heard, that my word must be kept, that one life must be bought with the other.

Even so, better, far better would it have been to let my child's white soul flutter heavenwards, than to retain it with my blood-stained hand.

But at that time my one thought was to save him, even though for his life, not one, but a thousand others had been immolated.

The day came when I was able to carry him in my arms from his cot to an easy chair beside the window. What a joy was that brief transit! His frail arms were round my neck and his head lay on my shoulder. With slow, lingering steps I went, loth to leave him out of my embrace.

A sweet Italian verse came light and fragrant into my memory:

I thought I bore a flower within my arms . . .

It was Prilukoff who reminded me with a cynical smile that the vow included also Nicolas Naumoff.

Nicolas Naumoff! I had almost forgotten him. Nicolas Naumoff! Must he, this distant and forgotten stranger, also die?

I cannot tell which of us it was who conceived the idea of making use of him as our instrument —of destroying him by making him a weapon of destruction, of murdering him by making him a murderer.

The idea may have been mine. I feared that I could not rely upon the languid, listless Prilukoff. Yes; it must have been I who devised this method of propitiating the avenging Fates, and averting from us the imminent Nemesis.

"A good idea," said Prilukoff wearily. "Let Naumoff do it." And he lighted a cigarette.

I gazed at him, aquiver with superstitious dread. "Do you think that then Naumoff need not die? Do you think that"—I hesitated—"*that* will be enough? . . ."

Prilukoff turned and looked at me as if aghast. Then he nodded his head and the fearful, crooked smile distorted his countenance.

"Yes," he said. "I think that will be enough."

XXXVIII

To what end should I narrate anew the terrible
story which is known to all? Must I dip again
into the soilure and abomination of that awful
time? How dare I tell of the luring telegrams
sent to the distant Naumoff, my guileless and im-
passioned lover, and of the joy and gratitude with
which he hastened to me? How describe the slow,
insidious poisoning of his mind against Kamarowsky, the hatred subtly instilled in him against
that unconscious, kindly man? And the lies, the
slanders, the ambiguous disclosures of pretended
outrages inflicted upon me, of insults and injuries
I feigned to have suffered at Kamarowsky's
hands? . . .

Naumoff believed it all. His astonishment and
indignation knew no bounds. What? Kamarowsky, whom he had always thought the most
chivalrous and considerate of men, was a despica-
ble, worthless coward? Well, Naumoff would
challenge him; he would fight a duel to the death
with him who had been his best friend.

But not that, not that was what I wanted.

Tioka recovered. Taller, thinner and paler, he came out once more into the sunshine, leaning on my arm, enraptured at everything, greeting every ray of light and every winged or flowering thing as if it were a new acquaintance.

Not for an instant did I suffer my mind to waver. God, the terrible God of my disordered fancy, had accepted the compact, and it was now for me to carry it out.

As soon as Tioka was well enough to travel, I sent him to Russia to some of our relations. While I was discharging my debt for his life, he must be far away.

Then began the ghastly game, the sinister comedy with the three puppets, whose strings I held in my fragile hands. I had to tranquilize and disarm Kamarowsky; to kindle and fan the murderous fury of Prilukoff; and above all to enchain and infatuate Naumoff, so as to impel him to the crime.

Ah, every art that Lilith, daughter of Eve and of the Serpent, has bequeathed to woman, every insidious perversity and subtle wile did I bring into play to charm and enamor this youthful dreamer. With every incitement did I lure and tempt him; with every witchery did I entangle him in the meshes of my perversity and in the whirlwind of my golden hair.

I was indeed the modern Circe, weaving her evil spell. I was fervent and temerarious, full of exotic anomalies, eccentric, unexpected. . . . I delighted in causing him both pleasure and suffering in a thousand unnatural and outrageous ways; I cut my initials in his arm with the triangular blade of a dagger; I pressed my lighted cigarette upon his hand; I assumed all the absurdities, perversities and puerilities with which since time immemorial woman has decoyed and beguiled man, who, after all, is essentially a simple-minded and ingenuous being.

Nicolas Naumoff was dazed and fascinated by all this strange hysteria and subtlety. He believed himself to be the hero of a fabulous passion —the incomparable conqueror of a wondrous and portentous love.

There were times when I myself was carried away by this play of my own invention. Now and then I lost sight of the grim purpose of this process of seduction; I rejoiced in my own coquetries, and myself burned in the flame I had deliberately kindled.

One evening as he knelt before me, pressing my cool hands against his fevered forehead, I bent over him with a smile.

"Why do you love me so much?" I asked. "Tell me. Tell me the truth."

He answered me gravely in a deep voice, enumerating the reasons on my fingers as he held them in his own.

"I love you because you are beautiful and terrible. Because you have that white, subtle face, and that mouth that is like a greedy rose, and those long, cruel eyes . . . I love you because you are different from all others, better or worse than all, more intelligent and more passionate than all." He was silent for a moment. "And also because you have forced me to love you."

Yes. I had forced him to love me. And now he was what I wanted him to be—an instrument ready to my hand: a fierce and docile instrument of death, a submissive and murderous weapon.

June crept warmly up from the south, and murmured of blue waters and dancing sunlight.

"Mura, let us go to Venice," said Paul Kamarowsky one afternoon as he sat beside me on the balcony; "let us pass these last three months of waiting at the Lido. If needs be, I can take you back to Russia later on, to complete the few formalities that must precede our marriage."

"To Venice?" I said faintly.

Paul Kamarowsky smiled.

"Ti guardo e palpito, Venezia mia,"

he quoted under his breath. And bending forward, he kissed my trembling lips.

XXXIX

WE prepared to leave. Naumoff's despair was puerile and clamorous. I entreated him to go back to Orel and wait for me there, and I promised him that I would soon return to Russia and see him again. As for Prilukoff, he awakened from his lethargy with the roar of a wounded wild beast. "To Venice! You are going to Venice with that man? Is that how you keep your vow?"

"I will keep it, I will keep it," I cried. "But I said—it—it should be done within the year—this is only June—we can wait six months longer."

"By that time you will be his wife," snarled Prilukoff between clenched teeth. "Unless it is done within the next three months you know it will never be done at all. Go your way," he jeered, "do as you like! Play fast and loose with fate as you have played fast and loose with me!" He turned and gripped my wrist. "But you will escape neither of us. Fate and I will overtake you, Marie Tarnowska, be it in Venice—or in hell!"

We left for the Lido.

And while, on the arm of my bethrothed, I wandered by the dancing waters, and the golden hours showered their light upon us, in my dark heart I prayed:

"God, give me strength and ruthlessness! God, who didst guide the hand of Judith, fill my soul with violence and teach my hand to slay!"

.   .   .   .

Prilukoff followed us to Verona. Then he came after us to Venice, where he took rooms in the same hotel, lurking in the corridors, shadowing us in the streets, pursuing me day and night with his misery and jealousy. Occasionally I saw him for a few moments alone, and then we would whisper together about the deed that was to be done, speaking feverishly in low quick tones like demented creatures. If I wavered, it was he who reminded me ruthlessly of my child and of my vow; if he hesitated, it was I who with the insensate perversity of madness urged him on towards the crime.

One evening—ah, how well do I remember that radiant summer sunset beneath which the lagoon lay like a fluid sheet of copper!—he met me on the Lido. He was morose and gloomy. He took from his pocket a black crumpled package. It was

Elise's old satchel—the "white elephant," tattered, empty, dead.

With a vehement movement he flung it into the water. Where it fell the sheet of copper shivered into a thousand splinters of red gold.

"Empty?" I asked in a low tone.

"Empty," he replied.

"And now, what will you do?"

He shrugged his shoulders. It was then that the idea came to him—the execrable, the nefarious idea.

"Listen. As he"—with a movement of his head he indicated the absent Kamarowsky—"is doomed—I suppose he is doomed, isn't he?" he interposed.

I assented in a barely audible whisper: "Yes."

"Well, his—his disappearance may as well be of some use. Do you not think so?"

Seeing the look of horror which I turned upon him, he continued: "For goodness' sake don't let us behave like romantic fools. We are not a pair of poetic assassins in a play, are we?"

Gradually, by subtle pleading and plausible argument, he led my weak brain to view the idea with less horror. He assured me that we had not only the right but almost the duty to commit this enormity. According to him, it was not a shame-

UNDER ARREST

ful and disgraceful deed. No; it was a just, reasonable, logical thing to do.

"Of course, it is not as if we were getting rid of a man simply in order to plunder him of his money. No, indeed. That would be vile, that would be abominable. But, given the necessity —the irrevocableness—of his fate, why should we not see to it that his death may at least be of some use to some one? Not to ourselves, remember. The money you get from him shall be used to serve a just purpose—to redress a wrong. We shall make restitution to those I have despoiled. I will pay back what I took from my clients to the very last farthing. And anything that is left over shall be given in charity to the poor. What do you say to that? We shall keep nothing for ourselves—nothing. Do you agree?"

He went on to recall that among the clients he had defrauded was a widow with four little children; the thought of her, he said, had always worried him. It was good to think that she would recover every penny.

The advocate in him awoke, eloquent and convincing, until he ended by assuring me that we should be performing a meritorious deed.

Indignant at first, then uncertain, then reluctant, I was finally persuaded. Soon I heard myself repeating after him: "It will be a meritorious deed."

Ah, if such beings as evil spirits exist, with what laughter must they have listened to our talk in that exquisite evening hour.

It was Prilukoff who thought out the details and settled the plan.

"You must get him to insure his life."

"How can I?" I cried feebly and tearfully. "How can one possibly suggest such a thing?"

"Leave that to me," said Prilukoff, reverting to his Moscow manner.

Next day he showed me a letter written by himself in a disguised hand.

"Open this letter when he is present, and when he insists on seeing it, show it to him . . . reluctantly!"

"But what if he does not insist?"

"You must make him insist," said Prilukoff.

The letter was brought to me in Kamarowsky's presence, and when he saw me turning scarlet and then pale as I opened it, he insisted on seeing what it contained.

I showed it to him . . . reluctantly.

The letter was in Prilukoff's handwriting, but was signed "Ivan Troubetzkoi." The prince (whom I scarcely remembered, and whom I had not seen for more than six years) begged me to marry him, and as proof of his devotion offered to make a will in my favor and, in addition, to insure his life for half a million francs.

Paul Kamarowsky was aghast.

"Is everybody trying to steal you away from me, Mura?" he exclaimed brokenly; then he sat down on the sofa with his head in his hands. I gazed at him, feeling as if I should die with sorrow and remorse.

For a long time he did not speak. Then he drew me to him.

"Dear one, do not heed the offers of other people. No one, whether he be prince or moujik, can love you more than I do. No one will do more for you than I am willing to do. I, also, am ready to make a will in your favor; I, also, will insure my life for half a million francs."

"No, no," I cried, crushed with misery and shame.

"Oh, yes, I will. It shall be done immediately. To-day."

And it was done.

"You see?" cried Prilukoff triumphantly, "I am not quite a fool yet, am I? Hush now, don't cry. Remember that it is not for ourselves, but to make an honorable act of restitution.''

''But a hundred thousand francs would have been enough for that,'' I sobbed.

''The other four hundred thousand we shall give to the poor,'' said Prilukoff. ''It will be a meritorious deed.''

XL

I REMEMBER that when I was a child I was taken
to a fair and given a ride on a switchback railway.
I was scarcely seated in the car, with the straps
round my waist and the giddy track before me,
than I cried to get out again. But the car was
already moving forward, slowly gliding down the
first incline.

I screamed, writhing against the straps, "Stop!
stop! I want to get out. I want to go back!"
But now the car was rushing giddily, in leaps and
bounds, down one slope and up another, whirling
over bridges and gulfs, dashing down the precipi-
tous declivity with ever-increasing speed.

Even thus had I embarked, almost without
realizing it, upon the rapid slope of crime. Impelled by my own madness, I had started on the
vertiginous course to perdition, and now I plunged
downwards, rolling, leaping, rushing into the darkness, without possibility of pause or return.

It was Kamarowsky himself who begged me
to leave Venice for Kieff, where some formalities

still remained to be accomplished before our impending marriage. He offered to accompany me, but I declined. He resigned himself, therefore, though with reluctance, to allowing me to start alone with Elise.

"Now," said Prilukoff, on the eve of my departure—and the transversal vein stood out like whipcord on his forehead—"let there be no more backing out and putting off. You will see Naumoff in Russia; send him straight back here. I'm sick of this business; let us get it over."

I bowed my head and wept.

Kamarowsky took me to the railway station, where I found the compartment he had reserved for me already filled with flowers. I thanked him with trembling lips.

"In three weeks, my love," he said, "you will be back again, and then I shall not part from you any more." He kissed me and stepped down upon the platform, where he stood gazing up at me with smiling eyes. Many people stood near, watching us. I leaned out of the carriage window, and as I looked at him I kept repeating to myself: "This is the last time I shall see him! The last time!"

It seemed strange and incongruous to see him there, with his usual aspect, making ordinary gestures and uttering commonplace remarks. Knowing as I did that he stood on the threshold of death, I wondered that he had not a more staid and solemn demeanor, slower, graver gestures and memorable words.

Whereas he was saying, with a smile: "Mind you don't lose your purse; and remember to look after your luggage at the Customs. You will have the dining-car at Bozen." And then, looking about him: "Would you like some newspapers?" He hurried away after the newsvendor, and then counted his change and argued about a coin which he thought was counterfeit. He came back to my carriage door, handed me the newspapers, and with his handkerchief dried his forehead and the inside of his hat.

"Fearfully hot," he said, looking up at me with a friendly laugh.

All this seemed terribly out of keeping with the tragic situation of which, all unconsciously, he was the hero. I tried to say something tender and affectionate to him, but my agitation stifled me.

"Mind you are good," he said, still smiling, and he threw a glance at some officers in the compartment next to mine.

I heard the doors being shut and the guard calling out *"Partenza!"* My heart began to beat wildly. I felt as if once again I were strapped in the car on the switchback railway. I wanted to get out, to stop, to turn back. A whistle sounded and a gong was struck.

"Well, Mura, *au revoir*," cried Kamarowsky, stretching up his hand to me. "A happy journey and all blessings."

I leaned out as far as I could—the bar across the window hindered me, but I managed to touch his outstretched hand with the tips of my fingers.

A spasm caught my throat. "Paul, Paul!" I gasped. "Oh, God, forgive me!" A shrill whistle drowned my voice as the train moved slowly forward.

He must have seen the anguish in my face, for he cried anxiously:

"What? What did you say?" Now he was running beside the train, which was beginning to go faster.

I repeated my cry: "Forgive me! Forgive me!" and stretched out my arms to him from the window.

He shook his head to show that he had not understood. The train was throbbing and hastening.

He ran faster beside it. "What—what is it? What did you say?" But the train was gaining speed, and he was obliged to stop. He stood there,

erect and solitary, at the extreme end of the platform, following with perplexed and questioning
gaze the train that was carrying me away.

It is thus always that I see him in my memory
—a solitary figure, gazing at me with perplexed
and wondering eyes.

Surely it is thus, thus wondering and perplexed,
that he must have looked in the face of death and
treachery, on that summer morning when he was
struck down by the hand of his friend.

The switchback plunges downward in its mad
race to the abyss—the end is near.

At Kieff, as arranged, I meet Naumoff.

I sob out my despair to him. Paul Kamarowsky must die. I give no reason, I explain nothing; I repeat unceasingly the three words: "He
must die," until there seem to be no other words
in the world—until the universe seems to ring
with those three words: "He must die!"

Naumoff recoils from me, pale-faced and horrified. Then I drive him from me, crying: "Go,
you are a coward. Let me never see you
again!"

"But why should he die?" cries Naumoff.
"What has the poor man done to you?"

Ah, what, indeed, has the poor man done?

Ramblingly, incoherently, I try to explain to

Naumoff; I tell him of Tioka and his illness, of my vow. . . . He listens amazed, without comprehending.

"But Mura, Mura! This is delirium, this is madness. You are ill, you are out of your mind. How can such an insensate idea possess you? How can you imagine that God would demand such an iniquity?"

Then I rack my brain for arguments that will convince him. I invent all manner of falsehoods; I repeat the tale of insults and outrages that I have endured at the hands of Kamarowsky; I accuse him of violence and brutality . . . and even as I tell these mad stories they seem to myself to be true. I am thrilled by my own words; I tremble, I weep convulsively; and Naumoff, ever more pale, ever more bewildered, does not know what to believe.

Continually, a dozen times a day, blind to all caution, reckless of all consequences, I send telegrams to Prilukoff—the telegrams that afterwards were found, and led to our arrest—"Berta refuses." (Prilukoff, I know not for what reason, had nicknamed Naumoff "Berta.") Then again: "Berta will do it." And again: "Berta irresolute. What am I to do?"

Then seized by sudden panic: "Wait! Do no

harm to any one. Advise me. Help me. I am going mad.''

Prilukoff telegraphs back his usual set phrase: ''Leave it to me.'' And he forthwith proceeds to send me a number of telegrams, all of which contain a series of insults and taunts addressed both to Naumoff and to myself. He signs them ''Paul Kamarowsky.'' Naumoff reads them in amazement, then in anger; finally he, too, becomes possessed of the idea of crime, obsessed by the frenzy of murder.

How can I tell the terrible story further? . . . The gust of madness caught us in its whirlwind, dashing us round like leaves blown in a storm.

One evening—it was a pale, clear twilight at the close of August—I sprang suddenly to my feet, and winding a black veil round my hair, I ran from my rooms and down the wide shallow flights of the hotel staircase. There were large mirrors on every landing. As I descended I saw at every turn a woman coming to meet me, a tall, spectral creature with a black veil tied round a white, desolate face . . . her light, wild eyes filled me with fear, and I hurried forward to reach the hall, where I heard voices and music.

Standing beside the piano in the vast lounge, two young girls were singing; they were English

girls, and they sang, with shy, cool voices, a duet
of Mendelssohn:

Fair Springtime bids the bluebells ring Sweet chimes o'er vale and lea

Some distance away, listening to them with
tranquil contentment on their peaceful faces,
sat their parents—the father, a stern, stately old
man with kindly eyes; the mother, gentle and
serene, wearing the white lace cap of renunciation
on her smooth gray hair. As I passed them with
faltering step the mother turned and looked at me.
What did she read in my face that wakened such
a look of tenderness and pity in hers? . . . She
smiled at me, and that smile seemed to stop my
heart, so guileless was it, so maternal and so kind.

For an instant a wild thought possessed me: to
stop, to fall upon my knees before this gentle, unknown woman and implore her help.

What if I cried out to her: "Help me, have
pity upon me! I am an unhappy creature whom
the Fates pursue. . . . I am distraught, I am demented—to-morrow I shall have murder on my
soul. Keep me near you . . . save me! Unless
you help me I am lost. . . ."

But the Furies that pursued me laughed aloud and lashed me forward.

And now Nicolas Naumoff, who had noticed my flight, came running down the staircase to follow me. . . .

I crossed the hall rapidly and went out into the dusk.

All in this mer-ry morn of Spring, Come out and dance with me.

XLI

THROUGH the twilight streets I hastened, and Naumoff followed, calling me by my name; but I did not answer him. Through the long Road of the Cross I hurried silently, and out through the Golden Gate, and on, down dusty solitary streets, past the Church of All Saints, until at last I stood before the cemetery where my mother is laid to rest.

"Where are we going?" asked Naumoff. "Why have you come here?"

But without answering him I threw a ruble to the gatekeeper and entered the silent pathways of the churchyard.

The sky was still light in the west, but the paths were gloomy in the shadow of willow and cypress trees. Hastening on between the double rows of flower-decked graves, and the monuments that gleamed whitely in the twilight, I reached my mother's tomb. I knelt and kissed the great marble cross that stands so heavily above her frail brow. And the thought of her lying there, so desolate and alone, abandoned to the rains and the winds and the darkness of long dreadful nights, struck terror to my heart.

"Speak to me, mother," I whispered to her. "Tell me what I am to do. You who know all —all about the vow and little Tioka, and the terrible things that are in my life—tell me, mother, must Paul Kamarowsky die?"

My mother did not answer.

"Tell me, tell me, mother! Is he to die?" My mother was silent. But the evening breeze passed over the delicate flowers, the lilies and campanulas which cover her grave; and they all nodded their heads, saying: "Yes, yes, yes."

"Did you see?" I whispered to Naumoff.

But he only looked at me with bewildered eyes. And I drew him away. "We must go quickly," I said.

Now it was growing dark. I hastened along the winding narrow pathways until in a deserted corner I found what I was seeking: a neglected grave marked by a gray stone bearing a name and a date.

As I gazed at that mound of earth, on which a long-since withered wreath spoke of forgetfulness, a wave of desolation swept over my heart. How sad and empty and useless was everything! Life and hope and love and desire—all empty, all unavailing. . . .

"Who is buried here?" asked Naumoff under his breath. He bent forward and read the name aloud: *"Vladimir Stahl."*

Something stirred. Perhaps it was only the dry leaves of the withered wreath, but I was afraid —afraid that I should see Stahl suddenly move and rise up, covered with mold, to answer to his name.

"Vladimir Stahl . . . " whispered Naumoff again, raising his haggard boyish face and gazing at me, "Mura, Mura, I see you encompassed by the dead."

Doubtless he meant the tombs which spread around me in a livid semicircle; but to me it seemed that he could discern standing behind me all my dead—my mother and Stahl, and Bozevsky and little Peter. . . . I uttered a scream as I looked fearfully behind me.

"Why do you scream?" gasped Naumoff; and he also turned and looked round. Then he pointed to the grave in front of us. "Who was this?" he asked in a low voice. "Did he love you?" His eyes flickered strangely. There was horror and lust and frenzy in the gaze he fixed upon me.

I was silent.

"Did he love you? Did he love you?" He

pressed closer to me, with parted lips and quickening breath.

Then I bent towards him, and a thrill such as I have never felt passed through me. "Swear—on the dead—that you will kill that man."

"I swear it," he gasped. "Terrible woman that you are, I swear it."

"Go," I whispered. "Go . . . at once." But he sprang towards me and fastened his lips upon mine.

Amid all the horrors that haunt my memory, all the spectral visions which drift darkly through the labyrinth of my life, that frenzied embrace among the tombs in the crepuscular cemetery, still rises before me—a ghost of darkness and of shame.

He turned and left me. I heard his footsteps running along the gravel path, I saw his tall shadowy figure vanish in the gloom. . . . He was gone.

I was alone in the nocturnal churchyard, alone by Stahl's desolate grave.

"Nicolas Naumoff!" I cried. But no one answered me, and fear ran into my heart with thudding steps.

I hurried forward, down the narrow path bordered with tombs and turned to the right, down another wider avenue among other endless

rows of the dead. . . . Where was I? In which
direction lay the gate? . . . I turned and ran
back. I must find Stahl's grave again, and then
go to the left through the unconsecrated burial-
ground of those who had died by their own hand.
. . . With shuddering breath I stumbled forward,
but nowhere could I find the dreary field of the
unshriven dead. Tall sepulchers and mausoleums
loomed dimly on either side of me, limitless rows
of tombstones and statues . . . but Stahl's low,
dreary mound was nowhere to be seen. Stay—
behind the willows on the right, was that not the
white cross standing on my mother's grave? . . .
To reach it quickly I left the pathway and ran
diagonally across the burial ground trampling the
graves in my haste to reach that large cross shim-
mering in the gloom. . . . No, it was not my
mother's grave. But further on, and further,
other crosses glimmered and beckoned—and I ran
on, crazed and terror-stricken, stumbling over
mounds and hillocks, tripping in iron railings,
trampling over flowers and wreaths . . . until I
fell in the darkness and lay unconscious and silent
amid the silent and unconscious dead.

. . . .

A breath of soft morning air awoke me. I
opened my eyes. Elise was bending over me with

pale and anxious face. The room—my bedroom —whirled and swam before my dizzy sight.

"Elise!" . . .

Elise Perrier clasped her hands. "Thank God!" she murmured. "I feared you would never wake again." Her face worked strangely, and she burst into tears.

"Elise—what has happened? What is to-day?" Before she could answer, another question sprang to my lips: "Where is Naumoff?"

"He has left, my lady," whispered Elise in awestruck tones.

"Left?" A long silence held us. "Left? Where has he gone?"

Elise looked down at me with blanched and quivering countenance.

"To Venice," she said in low tones.

I started up. "To Venice?" To Venice! My memory darted to and fro like a child playing hide and seek. "Elise! Elise! Elise!" I stretched out my hands like one sinking and drowning in the darkness. Elise wept. I watched the strange faces that Elise always made when she wept: funny, pitiful grimaces with puckered brow and chin.

"To Venice." My memory flickers like a feeble light, then blazes into sudden flames that sear my soul with fire. "Elise! He must be stopped. He must not reach Venice! Elise, stop him, stop him—!"

"It is impossible, my lady."

Yes, it is impossible.

(By this time the train which is carrying Naumoff on his mission of death has passed Warsaw and is hastening towards Brünn; hastening, ever hastening through the dawning hours and the noonday sunshine, hastening on into the twilight —and at dusk it rumbles and pants into the station at Vienna.)

I fall fainting back upon my pillows, and all through the day and the night I dream that I am speeding after the rushing train, catching up with it and losing it again, sweeping through the air, tearing along the unending rails, reaching it at last, and being struck down and crushed under its rolling wheels.

Day dawns once more.

"Elise, Elise, bring Naumoff back. Telegraph to him. Elise, for heaven's sake, bring him back!"

"It is hopeless, my lady."

Yes, it is hopeless.

(At this hour the train is hurrying from Botzen to Verona, from Verona to Vicenza, from Vicenza to Padua.)

Night falls on my despair.

. . . .

"Elise, Elise! Where are you? What is the time?"

"It is nearly dawn, my lady."

"Elise, what day is this?"

"It is the third day of September."

The third day of September!

"Elise," I scream suddenly, "Elise! Telegraph to Kamarowsky. Warn him. . . . Quickly, oh, quickly! Why, why did we not do so before?"

"Hush, my lady, hush! You were delirious; you could only rave and weep."

"Elise, Elise, telegraph to Kamarowsky. . . ."

"It is too late, my lady."

Yes, it is too late.

(At this very hour of dawn the train has reached Venice. Nicolas Naumoff is hastening from the Riva degli Schiavoni, across the empty piazza and the deserted streets. He hails a gondola. "Campo Santa Maria del Giglio!"

And the gondola, with soft plash of oar, glides slowly towards the doomed sleeper.

What dreams may the angel of rest have sent to him for the last time? Perhaps the tender vision of little Grania has gladdened him, while silent and inexorable in the closed gondola the youth with the golden eyes steals towards him through the mazes of the clear canals.

"Santa Maria del Giglio."

Nicolas Naumoff springs from the gondola, crosses the empty Campo and reaches the house. He ascends the steps quickly, knocks, enters—and closes the door behind him.)

Yes, it is too late.

I hear myself shrieking with laughter as I fall back on my pillows. Soon I am surrounded by strangers who hold me down, who thrust opiates between my lips, who lay soothing hands and cooling compresses on my brow. Then I know nothing more.

.   .   .   .

Elise Perrier's terrified face surges out of the darkness: she is speaking quickly, she is bending over me, imploring and urging. . . . What does she say? She weeps despairingly, and ever through her tears she speaks, urging and imploring.

Finally, in her thin arms, she drags me from my

bed; she dresses me; she wraps a cloak about me, and hurries backwards and forwards with traveling-bags and satchels. Now we are in a carriage —no, we are in a train. Elise Perrier sits opposite me, with ashen face and her hands in gray cotton gloves tightly folded. Her lips move. She is praying.

Suddenly I struggle to my feet: *"Paul! . . ."*

As I scream the name Elise springs upon me, covering my mouth with her cotton glove, pressing my head to her breast. "Silence! hush, hush, for the love of heaven! They will hear you. Hush!"

"Is he dead, Elise, is he dead?"

"No, no, he is not dead," gasps Elise in a toneless whisper, "he is not dead. We are going to him. He is wounded . . . he has been telegraphing to you for three days, begging you to come. And you would not move, you would not understand. . . ." Elise is crying again.

But perfect peace has descended into my soul. Paul is not dead. He lives! he lives! Nothing else matters but this—he lives.

The train still rushes along, beating rhythmic time to many tunes that are in my head; I gaze out of the window, at the whirling landscape that swings past like a giant chess-board, at the telegraph wires that dip, and then ascend slowly and dip again. Hours pass or days pass. . . . And the train stops.

Elise is hurriedly collecting cloaks and satchels. "Where are we, Elise? Are we in Venice?"

"Not yet; not yet. We are in Vienna."

As I step from the train, two men whom I do not know approach me. One of them asks me if I am the Countess Tarnowska. He has not taken his hat off, and I do not deign to reply.

As I am about to pass him he lays his hand on my arm. The other man also comes forward, and, one on each side, they conduct me along the platform. I notice many people stopping to look at me.

Nothing seems to matter. I do not remember why we are in Vienna, nor whither we are bound. I notice that it is a bright, hot day, and I feel that I am walking in a dream. . . . I find myself thinking of Vassili; I wish he would come, and send these men away and take me home. I shall be glad when I am at home with Vassili and the children and Aunt Sonia. . . . Safely at home!

Then I remember—I have no home. I am a forsaken, demented creature whom Vassili cares for no longer. But where am I going? I am going to Paul Kamarowsky, who lives and loves me! . . .

IN THE PRISON CELL

Again I weep with joy and thankfulness at the thought that Kamarowsky lives.

Now I am in a carriage driving through the streets of Vienna; and the two strange men are still with me. They are taking me to a hotel. We arrive. I pass through a large doorway and along some passages. Then I notice that it is not a hotel. It is a vast, bare room with wooden benches round the wall. Some men in uniform stand at the door, and I notice that they do not salute me when I enter.

Neither does an elderly man who is sitting at the desk rise or come to meet me. He looks at me steadily and asks me many questions; but I pay no heed to him. The windows are open; I can hear the sound of a piano very far away; somebody is practising a romance by Chaminade that I used to play at Otrada. . . . How sad a piano sounds when played by an unseen hand in the silence of a sunlit street!

The man at the desk speaks in German to the uniformed men; they take my golden wristbag from me, and conduct me out of the bare room down a long passage. As I go slowly forward between the two men I notice that from the far end of the passage a group of people are coming towards us. In the center of the group walks a man, handcuffed and wearing his hat crookedly at the back of his head, as if placed there by some other hand than his own. *It is Prilukoff!*

He sees me. A wave of livid pallor overspreads his face. Then he bends forward towards me and makes a movement with his lips, pressing them tightly together and shaking his head; he is trying to make me understand something. As they notice this the men at my side grasp my arm and make me turn quickly down another corridor. But I hear Prilukoff's voice shouting after me. He utters a Russian word: "Molci!" (Be silent).

The men thrust me rudely into an empty cell. I sit down on a bench fixed in a corner under the small, barred window and lean my head against the wall. I feel neither unhappy nor afraid; only weary, unspeakably weary; and almost at once I fall into a deep, dreamless sleep. Never since I was a child at Otrada have I known such perfect rest—such utter oblivion poured upon such limitless weariness.

Suddenly my door is opened abruptly and one of the men enters; he takes me by the arm, and conducts me back to the large, bare room, where the elderly official still sits at his desk. And there, standing before him, I see Elise. She is weeping bitterly. I see her making those comical

grimaces which always accompany her tears, as in
Italy cheerful music accompanies a child's funeral.
My mind—like a frightened bat that has flown into
a room and darts hither and thither—flutters and
plunges wildly through all my past life. I think
of my mother, of little Peter, and of Bozevsky; I
remember a pink dress I once wore here in Vienna,
at a reception of the Russian Embassy. . . . I
think of little Tioka and his days for saying
"No." . . . How far, how far away it all is!
What a gulf of guilt and sorrow have my tottering
footsteps traversed since then. . . . But now—
now I will climb tremblingly, devoutly, the steep
road that leads back to safety; hunbled to my
knees I will pour out my thanks. For Paul Kamarowsky is saved; he lives and will recover!

The man at my side is dragging me roughly
forward. The elderly official at the desk has beckoned to me, and as I stand before him in a line
with Elise he reads aloud from a sheet of foolscap.
Suddenly I hear the words: "Complicity in the
murder of Count Paul Kamarowsky. . . ."

The murder? *The murder!*

Two of the uniformed men hold my arms.

"But," I try to say, with chattering teeth,
"Count Kamarowsky lives . . . he will recover."

The man replies, "Count Kamarowsky is dead."

I laugh out loud. The car on the switchback rushes, whirls, plunges—falls with me to destruction.

XLII

Like a dream within a dream.—POE.

IT was in the prison infirmary that I first heard the details of what had passed in the Villa Santa Maria del Giglio, on that fatal morning of August the 3rd. As the nursing sister sat beside me, renewing from time to time the cold bandages placed on my throbbing forehead, she told me in low tones the mournful and tragic story. I listened as if I were listening in a dream to the story of a dream.

"When (she said) at early morning the Venetian servant-girl heard a knock at the door she went to open it, and a pale youth stepped quickly across the threshold. He asked for Count Kamarowsky, and bade the girl tell him that Nicolas Naumoff, of Orel, had arrived and desired to see him. The girl went to her master's door and knocked. He was awake and had risen. On hearing her message, he hurried out to meet his friend, for he loved him like a brother—"

("Ah, sister, I know, I know! He loved him like a brother!")

"When he saw Naumoff come in he went forward to meet him with open arms. The young man raised his hand and fired five shots point blank into his body. The Count fell to the ground; but even then he stretched out his arms to the young man and said: 'My friend, why have you done this to me? In what way have I ever harmed you?' The young man, with a cry as if he had awakened from a dream, flung himself on the ground at his feet. Then the wounded man showed him the balcony from which he might escape, and with fast-ebbing breath forgave him and bade him farewell."

("Oh, sister, sister, with fast-ebbing breath he forgave him and bade him farewell!")

"He was carried to the hospital, and the doctors wanted to give him chloroform while they probed the gaping, deep-seated wounds; but he would not take it. 'Do what you have to do without sending me to sleep,' he said. 'I shall have plenty of time to sleep—afterwards.' The doctors groped for the bullets in the lacerated flesh, and stitched up the five, deep-seated wounds. . . . When it was over he asked for you."

("Sister, sister, he asked for me!")

"He begged that you might be summoned quickly, and many telegrams were sent, but you neither came nor replied."

("I neither came nor replied!")

"On the third day he was better. He spoke to those around him, and again he asked for you, and hoped that you would come. In the hospital he was in the hands of an old and very famous surgeon; but alas! as Fate would have it—"

("What? what? As Fate would have it—?")

"As Fate would have it, the mind of this old and celebrated surgeon suddenly gave way. None knew that anything was amiss, as he stood that day at the bedside of the sufferer whom his skill had saved. He spoke to his assistants in the same calm, authoritative voice as usual, but he ordered that *the stitches should be taken out of the five wounds that were just beginning to heal.* Those around him recoiled in amazement. They were thunderstruck. But he repeated the disastrous order in the voice of one who is accustomed to command and to save lives that are in peril. Then—"

("What then? What then?")

"Then the assistants, doubting their own wisdom, but not that of the man who had been their master, obeyed, and reopened the five deep-seated wounds which were just beginning to heal. And again, as Fate would have it—"

(Ah, Fate! The ghoul, the vampire Fate! She who has pursued me since my birth! She who has caught us and crushed us all in her torturing grip, splintering us like frail glass bubbles in her hand! Now she had entered the sick room of Paul Kamarowsky, had brooded over his bedside, and in fiendish pleasantry had scourged the old surgeon's brain with madness, whipping it to frenzy as a child whips a top, guiding his hand to tear the injured body and reopen the fast-healing wounds.)

"As Fate would have it, the old surgeon gave other and still more dreadful orders. Ah, holy Virgin! how shall the horror be told? . . . When the bewildered assistants, aghast at what they had done, laid the sufferer back on his pillows, the slaying had been accomplished."

("The slaying had been accomplished!")

"With his last breath he called upon your name."

("With his last breath he called upon my name!")

THE PENITENTIARY AT TRANI

XLIII

E son quasi a l'estremo.
Luce degli anni miei, dove se'gita?

CARDUCCI.

IF I were to be asked to name the darkest hour of my dark life, well do I know which of all my gloomy memories would raise its spectral face.

Not the terror-haunted hours of madness and crime, not the anguish-stricken nights passed at the bedside of those I loved, not my own life-struggles with the monsters of disease and dementia, tearing at the very roots of my life—no, the darkest hour of my life was that glorious summer morning in Venice, when I was brought from the prison of La Giudecca to attend my trial at the Criminal Court. The sun flung a sparkling net of diamonds athwart the blue waters of the lagoon, and the gondola bore me with peaceful splash of oar over the dancing waters. The gondolier steadied the swaying skiff at the wave-kissed steps, and I rose, drawing my veil about me, to disembark.

As I placed my foot on the steps—how often be-

fore, in happier days, had I thus stepped from my
gondola, greeted and smiled upon by the kindly
Venetian idlers!—I lifted my eyes. A crowd had
assembled at the top of the steps and thronged the
piazza. They stood in serried ranks, menacing
and silent, leaving a narrow pathway for me to
pass. I faltered and would have stepped back, but
the carabinieri at my side held my arms and impelled me forward. At that moment some one in
the crowd—a woman—laughed. As if that sound
had shattered the spell that held them mute, the
mob broke into a tumult of noise, a storm of hisses
and cries, shrieks and jeers, hootings and maledictions, while, rising above it and more cruel than
all, was the laughter, the strident, mocking laughter that accompanied my every step and gesture.

And there, tall and motionless in the midst of
the laughing, hissing, shrieking mob, stood my
father, his white hair stirring in the breeze, his
eyes—the proud blue O'Rourke eyes—fixed upon
me.

Oh, father, father whose heart I have broken,
in that hour I paid the wages of my sin. Not these
dark years of imprisonment, not the mantle of
ignominy that clothes me with eternal defilement,
not the gloomy solitude in which I see the gradual

fading of my youth, not the horror of the past, nor
the hopelessness of the future—not these are the
deadliest of my punishments; but the memory of
your white hair in the crowd that hissed its hatred,
and laughed its contempt of your daughter, and
the jeers that greeted you, and the rude hands that
jostled you when you stepped forward and laid
your hand in blessing on my degraded head.

.   .   .   .

Marie Tarnowska is silent.   Her story is told.

EPILOGUE

The verdant landscape of Central Italy swings past the train that carries me homeward. The looped vines—like slim green dancers holding hands—speed backwards as we pass. Far behind me lies the white prison of Trani; and the memory of Marie Tarnowska and of her sins and woes drifts away from me, like some shipwrecked barque, storm-tossed and sinking, that I have gazed upon, powerless to help.

The long summer day is drawing to its close; above the Apennines where the sky is lightest the new moon floats like a little boat of amber on an opal sea. Like a fragment of a dream the song returns to my memory, the childish song of which I have never heard and shall never hear more than the first two lines:

> When little children sleep, the Virgin Mary
> Steps with white feet upon the crescent moon . . .

As the train carries me homeward, back to the joys of life and love and freedom, back to the welcome of friends and the safety of a sheltered hearth, I think once more of her whom I have left in the gloom of her prison cell.

Soon, very soon, the hour of her release will strike, and the iron doors that have guarded her will open wide to let her pass.

What then, what then, Marie Tarnowska?

Who will await you at the prison gate? Surely Grief, Scorn, and Hatred will be there. But by your side I seem to see a guardian spirit, shielding your drooping head with outstretched wings. It is the sister of lost Innocence—Repentance; and in her wake comes the blind singer, Hope.

THE END

1317292R0

Printed in Great Britain by
Amazon.co.uk, Ltd.,
Marston Gate.